LADY LAW

The Story of Arizona Supreme Court Justice Lorna Lockwood

by

D0483218

SONJA WHITE DAVID

Brighton Publishing LLC
501 W. Ray Road
Suite 4
Chandler, AZ 85225

LADY LAW

The Story of Arizona Supreme Court
Justice Lorna Lockwood

by

SONJA WHITE DAVID

Brighton Publishing LLC
501 W. Ray Road
Suite 4
Chandler, AZ 85225
www.BrightonPublishing.com

Copyright © 2012

ISBN13: 978-1-936587-92-6
ISBN10: 1-936-58792-0

First Edition

Printed in the United States of America

Cover Design by Tom Rodriguez

REVIEWS

"Packs a wallop in a small package." "The enchanting biographical story of Lockwood is interwoven with both historical context and legal concepts ..." "...author does an admirable job."

Book Review

by

Suzanne Dohrer

Maricopa Lawyer, the official publication of the Maricopa County Bar Association
July 2012 Volume 31 Number 7

"A compelling, informative, accessible and very engaging read. Lady Law follows Lorna Lockwood from childhood influences though her precedent-setting decisions on Arizona's Superior and Supreme Court benches."

Reader Review, Amazon

"This is a very interesting and well-written book. The reader will learn not only the story of Lorna Lockwood, but will also experience life in early Arizona. I highly recommend this book. Sonja has done a very good job researching and authoring!"

Reader Review, Amazon

"Brilliantly written inspiring story"

"I enjoyed this book very much. It is an intelligent, ambitious book which richly deserves high praise. In addition to telling the story of Lorna's triumph against overwhelming odds, it serves as an inspiration for achievment. Highly recommend."

Reader Review, Barnes & Noble

DEDICATION

To Richard

ᶜᐧᗖ *TABLE OF CONTENTS* ᗕᐧᵓ

✑ PREFACE ✐

The first time I saw Lorna Lockwood's name, it popped out at me from a big sample ballot pinned to a bulletin board in Chandler High School's gymnasium. I was with my mom and dad, who were there to vote. Lorna was running for judge of the Maricopa County Superior Court. Curiously, I don't remember any other name from that ballot. The year was 1950, I was ten years old, and Lorna won that election.

Ten years later, in 1960, I unexpectedly established a more personal connection to Lorna Lockwood. That was the year I joined a sorority, Chi Omega, at the University of Arizona. It was also the year Lorna ran—and won—the biggest campaign of her life, becoming the first woman ever elected to the Arizona Supreme Court. When I was initiated into Chi Omega, I was shown the chapter charter with the names of the fourteen founding members, one of which was Lorna Lockwood's.

As the years passed and I graduated from college, married, moved out of state, and raised a family, I forgot about Lorna. And then, in 1998, my husband retired and we returned to Arizona. During our very first spring back in the Grand Canyon State, my husband received a summons to jury duty. Soon after he reported to the Maricopa County Courthouse in Phoenix, he phoned me.

"Guess where I'm sitting?" he said. "In your sorority sister's room. The jury room is called the Lorna Lockwood room."

It still bears her name, a testament to her lasting influence.

I began to wonder about Lorna. Who was she? How did she achieve so much? I wanted to find out. One day I mentioned Lorna to an old friend, Eddie Basha. "Lorna's brother-in-law was our attorney," Eddie told me. "I'll introduce you to her family." And my journey began.

Lorna's family, particularly her nephews, Alfred Cox and Alan Cox, led me to some of her oldest friends, including lawyers, law clerks, and judges. Each one had favorite memories of Lorna, and as I listened, I began to feel as if I had known her.

Without exception, everyone I interviewed told me Lorna possessed such integrity, such brilliance as a judge, and what she accomplished for women was so groundbreaking that her story demanded to be told. As attorney Walter Cheifetz said, "Lorna deserves it."

⤳ *INTRODUCTION* ⤳

In the 1940s, a delegation from the Soroptimists and the Business and Professional Women's Clubs visited the governor of Arizona. They asked him to appoint Lorna Lockwood to fill a vacancy on the Maricopa County Superior Court. He refused their request.

"Lorna is a fine lady," the governor said, "and she may be a good lawyer. But no woman is capable of being a judge."

Lorna Lockwood proved the governor wrong. When she was elected to the superior court in 1950, she became the first female judge in Arizona. In 1960, she was the first woman elected to the Arizona State Supreme Court. And when she was selected as chief justice of that court in 1965, she became the first woman to achieve that position on any state supreme court in America.

In the twenty-first century, Lorna's achievement may not seem remarkable, but in the mid-twentieth century it was earth-shattering. How did she do it? To answer that question, we need to view her in her historical context, to understand the family into which she was born and the time and place in which she grew to adulthood.

As Lorna's first law clerk, Mark Harrison, said upon her retirement from the supreme court, "Perhaps her pioneering spirit is a by-product of the legal tradition in which she was reared. Her father was one of the handful of attorneys practicing in Tombstone not long after the Gunfight at the OK Corral."

Her father's influence cannot be overemphasized. By the time Lorna was ten years old she was determined to follow his example, which ultimately, she did—all the way to the state supreme court.

Lorna, however, was not a strident feminist. On the contrary, she was, in her own words, a lady. She had beautiful manners and was courteous to everyone. One of her favorite words was "polite." "You can say anything important," she told her young nieces and nephews, "as long as you say it politely. And it doesn't matter how old you are."

Still, even a tenacious spirit clothed in good manners rarely produces a Lorna Lockwood, and so the question remains—how did she do it? It all began in 1903, in the southeastern Arizona Territory where, a year earlier, a young couple had married and settled near the Mexican border.

Lady Law - Sonja White David

❧ CHAPTER ONE ❧

Pioneer Girl

On March 24, 1903, in the town of Douglas in the Arizona Territory, Daisy Maude Lincoln and Alfred Collins Lockwood expected, at any moment, the birth of their first child. "Please ask Harry to play something on the piano," Daisy begged her mother, Lorina Lincoln. "Something lively to lessen the pain!"

Mrs. Lincoln rushed to the parlor with her daughter's request. Daisy's cousin, Harry Hendrix, immediately sat down at the piano and tore into a popular two-step. Not long after that, a red-haired baby girl was born to the tune of "Creole Belle."

1

Daisy wanted to name the baby Lorina, after her mother. Alfred wanted to name her Elizabeth, after his own mother who had died when he was seventeen. They agreed on the two names but not on the order. "Lorina Elizabeth," Daisy said; "Elizabeth Lorina," Alfred insisted. The Presbyterian minister who had married the new parents, the Reverend Harvey Shields, came twenty-seven miles from the town of Bisbee to baptize the baby. "What will you name this child?" Reverend Shields asked as he dipped his hand into the water. "Lorina Elizabeth," Alfred announced, surprising everyone—most of all, his wife.

And so Lorina Elizabeth it was, on both the baptismal and birth certificates. But Lorina turned quickly into Lorna (Alfred loved Richard D. Blackmore's romantic novel *Lorna Doone*), and Lorna it would remain until the end of her days.

Alfred Lockwood, the eldest child of Walter and Elizabeth Peers Lockwood, was born in Ottawa, Illinois on July 20, 1875. At age seventeen, he developed a chronic cough and his physician recommended that he move to Idaho or Arizona. Alfred hated cold weather, and so immediately dismissed the idea of Idaho. But he

2

remembered the spring of 1886, when he was ten years old, traveling by train with his family across Arizona on a trip from Illinois to California. He'd been drawn to the warmer climate. Alfred's great-uncle, Ward Lockwood, had recently died and left five hundred dollars to Alfred and his four siblings, Lois, Lottie, Ralph, and Henry. So Alfred took his share of the inheritance and set out by train for Arizona, arriving in March, 1893. He described Phoenix as a "sleepy little village of four or five thousand inhabitants." The biggest building in town, three stories tall and made of brick, stood on the corner of Washington Street, and First Avenue.

That same year he sent for his mother (who was now divorced from Alfred's father) and his younger brothers and sisters. Soon after their arrival, Elizabeth—who was in poor health— died, leaving seventeen-year-old Alfred with four children to raise. (He would eventually put them all through college.) He did farm work for a while, and then bought his own ranch. While managing it, he studied at home for his teaching certificate. After passing the territorial exam, he taught for three years in the nearby Cartwright and Cave Creek schools.

Alfred's father and uncle were lawyers and, although he had never attended college or law school (only Collinsville High School), he knew he could "read the law" on his own, as had his future wife's distant cousin, Abraham Lincoln. He was encouraged to do so by a lawyer he'd met in the public library, where he liked to spend his rare free moments reading history. The lawyer, who was a graduate of Northwestern University's law school, acted as his mentor. Alfred was admitted to the Arizona Bar in 1902, the year before Lorna was born.

Lorna's mother, Daisy Maude Lincoln, settled in Douglas with her parents, Edgar and Lorina Lincoln, in 1901. Daisy was the town's first schoolteacher. Her brother Chester, who had come to Douglas earlier to work as an engineer for the El Paso and Southwestern Railroad, had recommended her for the position. Although Daisy was born in Santa Cruz, California, on March 12, 1877, she grew up in the Arizona Territory and graduated from Tempe Normal School (now Arizona State University) in 1899.

A few years prior to the move to Douglas, Daisy Maude was introduced to Alfred Lockwood by a mutual friend, Pearl Rigden, in Phoenix. The first time Alfred

4

saw Daisy, he was wearing his farm overalls and was too embarrassed to enter the Lincoln house.

As Alfred's grandson, Alan Cox tells the story, "Pearl insisted that he come inside and meet Mr. Lincoln's two daughters, Maude and Norma. He...relented and [entered] the broad hallway which ran through the [house]. He waited while Pearl went to the kitchen to get the girls. After considerable whispering and scuffling, the swinging door opened and both Lincoln girls emerged, blushing, alongside Pearl, who appeared quite triumphant. Alfred later learned that the Lincoln girls felt they were not presentable because they had been washing dishes."

Later, when Pearl asked Alfred what he thought of the girls, he said they were both nice, "but the older one, Maude, I'm going to marry someday if I can." And he did, on June 15, 1902.

The town of Douglas lies 118 miles southeast of Tucson, on the Mexican border. It was named for a Canadian mining engineer, James S. Douglas, who, in 1881, convinced the Phelps Dodge Company of New York to buy a Bisbee mine which became the Copper

Queen, one of the largest copper mines in the world. In 1901, Phelps Dodge built smelters in Douglas, where the copper was treated before it was taken to the El Paso and Southwestern Railroad Depot, loaded onto cars, and sent to eastern manufacturers.

Douglas, with its saloons, dance hall girls, gambling, and murders, was so unstable that in 1902, Captain Tom Rynning brought in his Arizona Rangers to keep the peace. "I've been in many a tough town…from Deadwood to Tombstone," Captain Rynning said, "but I've never met up with a harder formation than Douglas."

Alfred referred to their first home in Douglas as a "three-room shack." Later, as both his law practice (thanks to the mining industry) and his family grew (another girl, Charlotte, was born in 1907 and a boy, Chester in 1912), the Lockwoods moved up to a two-story adobe house.

One of Lorna's earliest photographs portrays her at four or five years of age. She is standing with a group of men posed behind a trophy which stands atop a coiled fire hose. The inscription names Lorna the "Mascot of the Douglas Hose Cart Team." The men were firefighters, and the horse-drawn cart (which is not pictured) carried hoses to fire scenes.

By 1910, Douglas had a population of 6,437. Three years earlier, because of the many mine owners and ranchers coming to town on business, Douglas built the five-story, 160-room Gadsden Hotel. The hotel, named after the Gadsden Purchase of 1853 which established the present border between Arizona and Mexico, was elegant, with a governor's suite, marble columns, and a grand staircase made of white Italian marble. It is said that the Mexican bandit-turned-revolutionary, Pancho Villa, once rode his horse into the lobby of the hotel and right up those marble steps.

Pancho Villa joined the Mexican Revolution when it began in 1910. He and his troops, the *Villistas*, fought throughout northern Mexico. The city of Agua Prieta lies directly across the border from Douglas. In the first battle of Agua Prieta, in April 1911, the revolutionary soldiers of Francisco Madero defeated the federal troops of dictator Porfirio Diaz, known as the *Federales*. Two weeks later the Federales took the city back. Madero's revolutionaries eventually forced Diaz to resign and go into exile, and Madero was elected president. But he was

7

assassinated in 1913 after having served only two years in office.

The Mexican Revolution went on for ten more violent years, and whenever it came near Agua Prieta, Douglas citizens who were not worried about stray bullets climbed to the tops of city buildings to watch. One evening, Lorna and her father were among those citizens.

"Are you kidding me?" said one of Lorna's friends when she told him this story many years later. "Going outside after dinner to watch a war?"

"No, I'm not kidding you," Lorna assured him, "we really did that."

Her sister Charlotte confirmed the story. Charlotte regretted that she was not allowed to go watch Pancho Villa fight because she was too little. Villa was a heroic figure to many people at the beginning of the Revolution because, like the English folk hero Robin Hood, he took from the rich and gave to the poor.

From an early age, Lorna wanted to help poor people. She was influenced by her grandmother, Lorina Lincoln. Mrs. Lincoln was, in Alfred's words, "soft-spoken and gentle, but very strong-willed." The daughter of a Christian minister, she taught her grandchildren how important it was to do the right thing and to help others, and the three Lockwood children took her lessons to heart. Over ninety years later, Charlotte said that throughout their lives, they "stood up for some very good things."

Lorna was eight years old when she was enrolled in the second grade at the local public school. Prior to this she was home-schooled. In addition to teaching her children how to read, Daisy Lockwood made certain they all learned to play the piano. She also taught them how to play basketball. Although, at that time, girls were thought to be too delicate to play more than half-court ball, Daisy taught them to play full court. Both Lorna and Charlotte went on to play basketball in high school and college.

But what Lorna loved most was to visit her father's law office and watch him at work. She adored her father and she wanted to do the things he did. "I thought it would be wonderful to be a lawyer and practice law with him," she said later.

On February 14, 1912, Valentine's Day, Arizona Territory became the State of Arizona. The following

9

year, when Lorna was ten, Alfred Lockwood was appointed judge of the Superior Court of Arizona for Cochise County. The Lockwood family left Douglas and moved forty-nine miles north to Tombstone, the county seat, where the courthouse was located. Now, instead of watching her father practice law in his office, Lorna observed him presiding over the courtroom. As a judge he made decisions that brought criminals to justice and justice to their victims.

"As I watched Dad I wished more than ever that I were old enough to sit on a bench and aid destitute families," Lorna stated many years later. Deeply affected by her father's judgments, it was in his Tombstone courtroom that she developed a passion for the rule of law.

Two other things influenced Lorna. First, in 1912, Arizona, Oregon, and Kansas, following the lead of six other Western states, gave women the right to vote, a right that most Eastern and Midwestern women would not receive until Congress passed the Nineteenth Amendment on August 20, 1920.

How was this possible? Because the new Arizona Constitution gave the people the power of initiative and referendum, which means that any citizen of the state— not only legislators at the capitol—may attempt to pass laws. This is done by initiating a law, printing it as petitions, and asking people to sign those petitions. If enough signatures are gathered, the proposed law is submitted to a referendum—a direct vote of the people. If the majority approves, it becomes law. The Woman's Suffrage movement was so strong in Arizona that, using the power of initiative and referendum, suffragists convinced male citizens to extend the right to vote to women.

The second important event Lorna's family would have talked about was another achievement for women. In 1913, Sarah Herring Sorin, the first woman to practice law in Arizona, became the first woman to argue a case before the United States Supreme Court without assistance from a male colleague. She had practiced mining law in Tombstone with her father in the 1890s. Although Sorin and her father moved their practice to Tucson before the Lockwoods arrived in Tombstone, her story had become part of the town's history. Lorna saw in

11

Sarah Sorin a clear example of what she herself could achieve.

Tombstone was a frontier town created by the mining boom which began in 1877, when a prospector by the name of Ed Schieffelin struck silver. Because roving gangs of outlaw cowboys were smuggling in cattle from Mexico, the area was considered so dangerous that before Schieffelin left the Army's Camp Huachuca to go prospecting, he was told that the only rock he would find would be his own tombstone—hence the town's name. Schieffelin's strike was followed by the discovery of some of Arizona's richest mines, including the Lucky Cuss, the Toughnut, and the Owl's Nest.

By 1881, the year of the famous Gunfight at the OK Corral between the Earps and the Clantons, Tombstone had a population of 10,000. It also had a newspaper, *The Tombstone Epitaph*, published by Tombstone's mayor, John P. Clum; a school; four churches; and over 100 saloons, including the famous Bird Cage Theater, which opened on Christmas Day of that year. *The New York Times* reported that the Bird Cage was "the wildest, wickedest night spot between Basin Street and the Barbary Coast."

There were nightly shootings. Tombstone was considered to be the "toughest town in the nation." George Whitehall Parsons, who kept a diary of Tombstone life from 1880–1887, wrote of the danger of raiding cowboys shooting down innocent people and recorded "14 murders and assassinations in 10 days." Saloons and gambling were a deadly combination. On February 25, 1881 at the Oriental Saloon, in retaliation against verbal insults, frontiersman Luke Short, despite deputy Bat Masterson's attempt to stop him, shot professional gambler Charlie Storms in the heart.

There was much violence—so much, in fact, that the city council banned guns in town—but there were also church groups and bazaars, ice cream socials, and pageants. The respectable ladies who organized these activities did not associate with dance hall girls and cowboys. However, it was not always easy to tell the difference between the respectable and the not-so-respectable. Historian Edward Peplow writes that the stories of the Earp Brothers, Doc Holliday, and the Clantons "have been told and retold to the point where...it is difficult to decide who among them was good [and] who was bad." But one thing was certain; an honest cattleman never referred to himself as a cowboy. He was a herder or a rancher. To call him a cowboy was to call him "a horse thief, a robber, and an outlaw."

By the time the Lockwood family arrived in Tombstone the population had decreased to about seven hundred. In 1886, the mines filled with water when the main pump burned down, and the mining industry came to an end. But all was not peaceful. As late as 1919, according to the *Arizona Republic*, "the secretary of the Arizona Livestock Board reported that Cochise County was swarming with cattle rustlers." Tombstone remained important; the two-story, red-brick courthouse, built in 1882, continued to be the center of law and order for the county. The Lockwoods lived across the street from it. Unlike the Douglas house, made of adobe that kept them cool in the summer and warm in the winter, the Tombstone house was built of wood and not so well insulated against the weather. It had three bedrooms, but no plumbing and so no indoor bathroom; instead, there was an outhouse in the backyard.

Water had to be pumped from an outdoor well, hauled into the kitchen, and heated on the wood stove. It was then poured into a metal pan for washing dishes or

14

into a small ceramic basin for bathing—one body part at a time. A real bath was a luxury, because filling a portable tin bathtub required hauling and heating fifteen or twenty gallons of water. In good weather, laundry was done outdoors. All clothing, sheets, and towels were scrubbed by hand with soap on a washboard in one tub of water, and then rinsed clean in another.

Housekeeping was women's work, and that work was difficult. In 1916, when Lorna was thirteen years old, she was kept home from school for a year for the purpose of learning how to keep house. Judge Alfred Lockwood believed girls should know how to manage a household. In addition to doing the laundry and cleaning, Lorna planned three meals daily, shopped for groceries, and did all of the cooking.

Few careers other than teaching and nursing were available to women, and even those were rarely open to married women. If a schoolteacher or nurse married, she was usually required to quit her job. Women were expected to marry and raise children. Lorna grew up with the belief that she could have marriage or a career, but not both. She learned to cook well, and to keep a good house, but she was quite certain about the life she wanted by the time she was ten years old.

Although Alfred and Daisy's beliefs about the role of women were conventional for the early-twentieth century, they were unconventional in another respect; at a time when children were to be seen and not heard, Alfred and Daisy not only encouraged but also expected their children to express their opinions, and to support those opinions with facts. There were lively discussions at the dinner table, some of which became loud arguments during which their mother had to intervene and remind them to be polite.

Lorna's sister Charlotte recalled how one of those discussions taught her to think more carefully. Charlotte's best friend in Tombstone was a girl whose grandfather had fought for the Confederacy in the Civil War. One evening at the dinner table, Charlotte announced that she had something important to tell them, something new she had learned from her friend.

"Everyone has the wrong idea about how slaves were treated in the South," Charlotte said. "Most of the slaves were never beaten. They were well-fed and their

16

masters gave them clothes. They gave them a place to live. Their masters treated them well."

Alfred, whose maternal grandfather, as part of the Underground Railroad in southern Illinois, had helped runaway slaves from the South escape to Canada, looked carefully at Charlotte. And then he said just one thing: "They treated their slaves just the way you would treat your dog." Her father had not argued with her or tried to talk her out of her viewpoint; instead, with one sentence, he created a picture which caused his daughter to ask herself if she really believed that human beings who happened to be black were no better than dogs. She remembered that as one of the most important lessons of her life.

The dinner table discussions, during which everyone was expected to contribute, continued as long as the family was together. The discussions helped develop the Lockwood children's intellects, teaching them to ask questions and think for themselves.

When Lorna entered Tombstone High School she was well-prepared to be a serious and thoughtful student. She excelled in academics, played cello in the school orchestra, and, for fun, played girls' basketball. Lorna graduated from Tombstone High School in 1920, one of a class of nine. She registered at the University of Arizona in Tucson, took up residence in North Hall, and studied pre-law in addition to Spanish and psychology.

Although Lorna worked hard and, by going to summer school, graduated in three years instead of four, she still participated in many activities. The mascot of the University of Arizona is the Wildcat, and Lorna was a proud one. A natural leader, she played on the women's basketball team, ran on the women's track team, and organized the women's chorus. She was also named the outstanding reporter on the university newspaper, the *Arizona Wildcat.*

Lorna took an important step at the University of Arizona in 1921, one which would lay the foundation for what would become a political career. She and some friends formed a local sorority which they called Chi Delta Phi. In 1922, when their local group was accepted into the national collegiate sorority Chi Omega, Lorna was one of the fourteen founding members. Her power base was born.

"Oh, what fun we had, all the Chi Omega sisters," Marjorie Blackman wrote, over seventy years later, of her own 1928 pledge class. They went to rodeo dances, rode horses, had picnics in the desert, rode the streetcar downtown to the movies, and bought hot tamales for a dime. "And the friendships," she continued, "last a lifetime." Indeed they did. As a Chi Omega, Lorna discovered that sisterhood is powerful. She later said it was while she was in college that she first decided she would one day run for the state legislature. Following the example of her mother, Daisy, who helped establish the women's clubs in Douglas and Tombstone, Lorna joined many women's organizations. These organizations, which she called her "base of support," became the backbone of her political success.

Lorna was front-page news in her hometown newspaper, the *Tombstone Epitaph*, on April 1, 1923. "Tombstone Girl Honor Candidate of Phi Kappa Phi," the paper proudly announced. Lorna was one of only seven students in the graduating class to be initiated into the honor society. However, when Lorna tried to enter the University of Arizona Law School, which had been established in 1915, she ran into serious opposition.

19

"Law school is no place for a woman," Dean Samuel Fegtly told Lorna. She returned again and again to the dean's office, but he would not change his mind. Lorna said "the dean did everything he could to dissuade me from pursuing a law degree." He reminded her that only two women practiced law in the state at the time. What chance could Lorna possibly have for any kind of law career? He thought she should become a secretary. But she refused to give up, and eventually she brought in her father, the Tombstone judge, to help argue her case. The dean gave in.

"So I went into the law school," Lorna said, "and I was very timid. After all, I was the only girl in the class and, remember, that this was right after World War I and there were a lot of returning soldiers and they were considerably older than I."

Lorna may have been shy about being the only woman in a class with twelve men, but she was elected president of the Student Bar Association. It was probably the only election in her life she ever won without another woman's vote!

There were times when Lorna felt awkward in her classes. In 1924, women were thought to be too delicate to be exposed to certain subjects such as, of all things, cow manure. One day, the professor asked each student to present one of the lawsuits from the assigned reading to the rest of the class. He went down the list and assigned the cow manure case to Lorna. She blushed. She was embarrassed, and so was the rest of the class, but she carried on and talked her way through it. After class, the professor told Lorna's classmate, Renz Jennings (who would one day sit on the state supreme court), that he was mortified to have assigned that case to the only woman in the class. He had not been thinking!

The idea that certain topics should not be discussed when women were present prevailed at the law school for years. For example, women were excused from the classroom whenever the case under discussion was related to sexual assault. It was assumed that should a woman actually become a lawyer she would confine her work to "respectable" cases. Even in the 1940s, a Phoenix attorney said that because there were some things that could not be discussed in front of women, he was quite worried about how to present certain cases in court, should a woman be on the jury.

Lorna was twenty-two when she graduated from the University of Arizona Law School in the class of 1925, which was the last class to be admitted to the State Bar of Arizona without taking an examination. Although Lorna was the second woman to graduate from the U of A with a law degree—the first was Lucy Stanton in 1921— she was the first woman, and the only member of her class, to be awarded a JD, the Juris Doctor degree. The other twelve members—all men—were awarded an LL.B., the Bachelor of Laws degree, which means they had not earned undergraduate degrees before entering law school. At the time this was not unusual. Lorna *was* unusual in that she had been awarded a bachelor of science before beginning her law studies. The juris doctor was not only a graduate degree; it was also a professional degree. In the graduation program Lorna is the only law school graduate listed under "Professional Degree."

Lorna's sister Charlotte said that Dean Fegtly complimented Lorna in his graduation speech. He referred to her as not only a daughter of the university, but also a daughter "in law"!

"I think he was proud of me," Lorna said.

Throughout her life Lorna remained a loyal Wildcat, and the U of A returned that loyalty. The U of A later honored her with the Alumni Achievement Award, the Distinguished Citizen Award, and the Medallion of Merit. Years later, university president Richard Harvill wrote the following to Lorna: "We are happy that you are recognized as the first woman to become Chief Justice of a supreme court in the United States, and we are delighted that you are a native-born daughter of Arizona. It is a particular source of joy that you are an Alumna of the University of Arizona."

But those honors were far in the future. It was 1925, and things looked bleak. Lorna Lockwood, who had been admitted to the State Bar of Arizona on June 4, could not find a job. It would be fourteen years before she could practice law.

୫୬ *CHAPTER TWO* ୬୭

Lady in Waiting

"**M**y original plan when I finished law school was to go into private practice with my father," Lorna said. "I thought that by the time I finished school, his term as a superior court judge in Cochise County would be over and he might be willing to open an office with me. But, he fooled me. He ran for the [Arizona] Supreme Court and won."

In 1925, law firms rarely hired female lawyers. The one way a woman could practice law was to go into her father's or brother's law firm, as Sarah Sorin had done in Tombstone years before. Lorna could not practice law with her father because judges—or justices, as they are called on a supreme court—no longer practice as lawyers. Judges and justices instead listen to the arguments of lawyers and make judgments as wisely and fairly as they are able.

The Arizona Supreme Court is located in the capital, so the Lockwood family moved to Phoenix and built a two-story, four-bedroom house at 84 West Cypress Street, six blocks north of McDowell Road and a block and a half west of Central Avenue. With the exception of an occasional apartment, this was Lorna's home for the rest of her life.

Years later, Lorna said that her career was "fortuitous, not planned in definite steps." Her father told her that "opportunity knocks at everyone's door, but the person sitting on the doorstep is the one who is able to grasp the opportunity."

For the next fourteen years, Lorna sat on a lot of doorsteps.

She started out by working as her father's secretary and law clerk at the supreme court. It was, for her, the next best thing to practicing law. But in 1932, the legislature passed an anti-nepotism law. Nepotism refers to people, usually in public office, who give jobs to their relatives. This new law meant that Lorna could no longer work for her father and had to look for another job. She found a position as a legal secretary for the law firm of Armstrong, Kramer, Morrison, and Roche.

Being Lorna, she did not confine her activities to her job. She joined the Eastern Star and became a leader for the Campfire Girls. She taught Sunday school at the First Congregational Church, where she was a founding member. She joined every women's club she could find and was eventually elected local or state president of them all. She worked her way up in the Democratic Party, from precinct level to the vice-presidency of the state central committee.

In 1938, when Lorna was thirty-five years old, she gathered her courage and made an important decision.

27

She informed the director of the law firm that she would no longer work as his secretary because she wanted to run for the state legislature. The director did not believe she could win. According to Lorna, her boss "was a little reluctant and finally he said 'Well, you can do that but remember you'll always have a place here if you want to come back.'" She never did.

Lorna won that election, and it changed her life forever. In 1939, she took her place in the Fourteenth Legislature, established a private law practice with Loretta Savage, and was admitted to practice law—argue cases—before the United States District Court.

The two lawyers worked hard to build their practice. They rented a small room on the fourth floor of the Luhrs Tower in downtown Phoenix and took any case they could get. Sometimes their male colleagues felt sorry for Lorna and Loretta and referred clients to them.

Lorna's sister, Charlotte, who was now married, occasionally came in to help with secretarial work. This was not a great success because Charlotte had to bring her five-year-old son Alfred with her. To keep him busy, Loretta gave the boy a large pile of paper clips and showed him how to string them into a chain. He recalled that while the stringing part was fun, the unstringing was boring, so Loretta had to spend more time taking the paper clips apart than Alfred had taken to put them together. The next secretarial help Lorna and Loretta hired was a young man who was a student at the Gregg Shorthand School. During the single month they were able to afford his services, their male colleagues laughed at them. Imagine, two lady lawyers with a male secretary!

Loretta said they almost "starved to death." In 1942, they dissolved the partnership.

Lorna's career in the Fourteenth Legislature was more successful. She represented District 18, which was made up of the Los Olivos, Isaacs, and Christy Precincts in Phoenix.

Six weeks into her first term, Lorna and another legislator, Marvin E. Smith, spoke to the Democratic Woman's Club at the Adams Hotel in Phoenix. On February 20, 1939, the *Arizona Republic* reported that Lorna "showed a keen understanding" when presenting the pros and cons of the civil service reform bill she had introduced to the legislature. Marvin Smith did not appear to know much about the bill "and therefore digressed from his assignment" and rambled on about how "women could divert their energies in the cause of legislation."

Lorna's bill did not pass, but she was not discouraged. She continued to work for a merit system in state government. She wanted state employees to be hired because they were competent and not because they had contributed money towards the elections of government officials.

In May of 1940, Lorna announced her re-election campaign in the *Arizona Republic* and the *Phoenix Gazette*. She said she would work to revise the tax system "so that its burdens will be more equitably distributed." She also wanted to provide more assistance to the elderly and others in need "to the greatest degree consistent with sound economic government."

Lorna's campaign-poster photograph shows her with wavy hair pulled back and a hint of a smile on her lips. She looks focused, confident, and determined—the qualities that would, for a second time, carry her to victory.

During Lorna's first two terms, she produced thirteen bills independently. Her work on legislation for better health care culminated in the creation of a new state board of health. She served on several committees, including Child Welfare, Education, Public Health, Highways and Bridges, Banking and Insurance, Constitutional Amendments, Referendum and Rules, and—most important to her—the Judiciary Committee, which she chaired. As the *Mesa Tribune* later reported, "The feminine legislator rapidly acquired the reputation for getting things done."

In 1940, Lorna was one of seventy-five women invited to the White House by First Lady Eleanor Roosevelt to help organize the campaign to fight polio (infantile paralysis, as it was known at the time). It was a devastating disease for which there was neither a vaccine nor a cure. The disease killed thousands and crippled thousands more, including President Franklin Roosevelt, who struggled valiantly but in vain to regain the ability to walk. As Arizona's representative to this campaign, Lorna attended a tea hosted by Mrs. Roosevelt at the White House. She also attended a dinner in honor of the First

Lady at the Carlton Hotel. This was Lorna's introduction to Washington, D.C.

In 1942, at the end of the Fifteenth Legislature's regular session, Lorna returned to Washington as the assistant to Arizona's only congressman, John R. Murdock. She had met Congressman Murdock years before when he taught one of her summer classes at the U of A.

A few months earlier, in December 1941, the United States entered World War II after the Japanese bombing of Pearl Harbor. Many young women went to Washington to fill jobs vacated by men who were fighting in the Pacific and European theaters. When the congressman invited Lorna to be an aide in his office, she knew it was her chance to help the war effort. Met by the congressman's wife at Washington's Union Station on a bright spring day, Lorna saw sun shining on the dome of the United States Capitol and thought it was beautiful. "I…want to thank someone for this Arizona sunshine that has given me such a warm welcome to my nation's capital," she said.

Mrs. Murdock took Lorna to a "stately red brick mansion" across from the Supreme Court. It had been the home of Alice Paul, the suffragist, but now belonged to the National Woman's Party. It rented rooms to women, and Mrs. Murdock had been lucky to find one for Lorna, who was delighted to discover that hers was filled with antiques, including a crystal chandelier and a big bed with a canopy.

As usual, Lorna did not waste time. Any attorney who is a member of the bar of the highest court in any state may apply to practice law before the United States Supreme Court, and on May 11, Lorna's application was accepted. She could now argue a case before the highest court in the land. She also "learned a lot about Congress and how it worked." After a year and a half in Washington, however, Lorna seemed anxious to return to Arizona, which she called "the best state in the nation." She would never again live anywhere else, and she was completely committed to its welfare for the rest of her life.

Returning home in 1944, Lorna became the chief attorney for the Office of Price Administration, a temporary agency which was established to prevent wartime inflation. She worked under Richard A. Harvill, who was later appointed the president of the U of A.

After the war ended in 1945, Lorna finally achieved her childhood goal of going into private law practice with her father, who had retired from the state supreme court in 1942. They joined Charlotte's husband, Simpson Cox, in the firm of Cox, Lockwood, and Lockwood. The following year, Lorna ran for a third term in the Arizona State Legislature and won, taking her seat in the Eighteenth Legislature in January, 1947.

Lorna applied for membership in the Lawyer's Club of Phoenix, but was rejected. The club did not admit women. Lorna did not challenge the decision, but she never forgot that injustice. Instead, she quietly formed her own club for women lawyers—although she did not call it that. She had a standing lunch reservation each Wednesday at The Flame, a popular meeting place for lawyers in downtown Phoenix. Lorna told all the women lawyers in town they were welcome to show up anytime. There were so few, only five or six, that all could fit at a single, round table. The male lawyers were sure to notice their female colleagues at the same table week after week.

"We used to network," attorney Virginia Hash stated, "long before [we] ever heard of such a thing" Virginia remembered that although she graduated from law school more than twenty years after Lorna, things were still no better for women. Law firms would not hire them, so Virginia went to work in her uncle's firm. "I remember walking into court in the early years and being treated like a secretary," she said. She had, however, no intention of being anyone's secretary, and she let no one know she could take shorthand.

Before Virginia met Lorna, she imagined that because of Lorna's name she would be "tall, sylph-like, and splendid," She was surprised to find, instead, a woman she described as a "short, dumpy redhead." Virginia was still in law school when she met Lorna, who had already established a career in politics as well as the law. Their personalities could not have been more different; Lorna was formal and dignified, Virginia feisty and irreverent. In spite of that they became the best of friends.

Virginia liked to use a "psychological tool" against male opponents in the courtroom. She stared at their shoes and socks. She said that one man "wore the darndest fluorescent socks…that used to shine brightly, and I'd stare at them in utter fascination and get him so upset."

"But if you were a woman," Virginia said, "you never crowed when you beat him. If you did you were in trouble. I learned it *real* early!"

In 1949, at the end of Lorna's third term in the legislature, she was appointed assistant attorney general for the State of Arizona. She was the only woman among several assistants, one of whom, J. Edward "Bud" Jacobson, became a good friend.

That same year, Attorney General Fred O. Wilson came under investigation for fraud. Mr. Wilson was accused of "selling opinions" of the attorney general's office—in other words, taking bribes for writing opinions that would make certain persons or businesses rich. Bud said there was a "black cloud" hanging over the office. The young assistants "huddled under this cloud" and worried they would be tainted by it; most tried to distance themselves from the attorney general. Bud asked Lorna if Wilson had ever told her what to write or to change an opinion once she'd written it.

"No," she said, "he has not."

"He hasn't asked me to, either," Bud told her.

Bud and Lorna could find no evidence that Mr. Wilson had taken bribes. They agreed to testify on the attorney general's behalf, even though he had not asked them to. The other assistants warned them that they should not testify because it might hurt their careers.

"That doesn't matter," Lorna said. "It's the right thing to do."

"So," Bud said, "Lorna and I made an outing of it. We drove down to Yuma in my new convertible, because the trial was being held in the Yuma County Courthouse, and we testified. And then we ate at some great Mexican restaurant."

The attorney general was found not guilty.

On weekends, Lorna, Bud, and their friends gathered for cook-outs on the big flagstone patio behind Bud's house on Clarendon Street. They sat on a bench, large enough to hold thirty people, built around an enormous eucalyptus tree. During one of these parties Lorna announced that she would like to run for judge of the superior court. She asked her friends what they thought, because no woman had ever run for that office.

"Of course, I think she'd already made up her mind," Bud said, "but she liked to make us think she was asking our opinion. She made history right there in my backyard by announcing her political plans to our friends and some of my neighbors from up and down the street—as well as to the *zanjero*, or ditch boss—who arrived from the Salt River Project at that very moment to open my irrigation gates to water the lawn!"

Lorna knew many people would be prejudiced and not vote for her because of her sex. She told Virginia she thought she would have a better chance of winning the election if she campaigned to be a juvenile judge. She was already a member of the board of the Maricopa County Juvenile Detention Home, as well as the Maricopa County Youth Committee. She remarked that it might be easier for people to think of a woman judge who dealt only with juveniles, rather than with hard core criminals. Women, after all, were supposed to be motherly, soft, and feminine. Virginia did not like that idea at all.

"If you're going to be a judge," she told Lorna in her usual forthright manner, "be a *judge!*"

This was Lorna's fourth election, and she was getting to be a clever campaigner. She was one of thirteen candidates running for five seats on the Maricopa County Superior Court. During the campaign, all thirteen appeared together and took turns speaking. When it was Lorna's turn she stood up, looked out carefully over her audience, and said "I know most of you have already decided upon your first choice, and that's fine. I know most of you already have your second choice, and that's fine, too. And I know most of you have your third choice. What I'm asking is that you make me your fourth choice."

When Lorna sat down, one of her opponents turned to another and said, "Well, you and I may be the second and third choices, but I'll tell you who's going to be the number one choice, and that's Lorna Lockwood!"

Lorna did not place first, but the voters granted her request; she came in fourth, knocking two sitting judges off the bench.

"I believed when I decided to run for judge," she told the *Phoenix Gazette*, "the people of the county wanted a woman on the bench. Apparently, looking at the results of the voting, I was right."

Lorna's upset victory gave Arizona its first woman judge.

ᑫᕊ CHAPTER THREE ᕊᑐ

Lady Law

"**I** remember the first day she was on the bench," Virginia Hash said of that January, 1951 event. "Her father was still alive and he came down to watch her. He was the proudest man. He should have been. Women just didn't do those things in those days!"

"She's going to do all right," said Alfred Lockwood after he left his daughter's courtroom. "She's going to be OK."

How grateful Lorna must have been that her father, whom she had emulated all her life, lived to see

41

her as the state's first woman judge! Alfred died a few months later, on October 30, 1951, still deeply mourning Lorna's mother, Daisy, who had died on November 17th of the previous year.

If Virginia's first impression of Lorna years before was of a "short, dumpy redhead," another colleague, a male, saw her in a different light: "I would describe Lorna as attractive," recalled Lorna's first law clerk, Mark Harrison, "although undeniably plump..." She had a very pretty face, piercing eyes, and a very animated persona. She also had a good sense of humor and that was part of her success. In contrast, she did not suffer fools gladly and did not respond well to phonies or lawyers who didn't live up to their professional obligations."

And, in addition, that black judicial robe increased her aura of dignity and authority. From the very beginning, Lorna controlled her court room.

"I decided that I would run the court in accordance with the law," she said, "and there were two lawyers, rather prominent lawyers, who were very contentious...they would jump up and interrupt each other...I knew that wasn't proper. And I reprimanded them, but they continued. Finally, I rapped the gavel and said 'Gentlemen, I find you both in contempt and fine you five dollars. You may pay the clerk.' Well, that stopped everything. One of them stepped up to me and said 'Well, I don't have the cash. Could I pay later?' I said 'Yes.' There was a room full of lawyers and they all laughed, and it was all over. I never had any trouble after that."

One of those lawyers, Jack Cavness, had been defeated by Lorna for a seat on the superior court the year before; the other, W. Francis Wilson, was president of the Maricopa County Bar Association. Perhaps they resented having to try their case before a female judge—especially a woman who had bested one of them in an election. But, whatever the reason, acting as if they were on a school playground instead of in a courtroom did not have the desired result. They did not undermine Lorna Lockwood.

Soon after "the incident of the contentious lawyers," Lorna was tested by a young man from a prominent family who boasted that he could talk his way out of anything. When he appeared before Judge Lockwood on a serious traffic charge, he promised, with his usual breezy confidence, that he would never break that law again.

"Well, you won't break it again for the next six months," the judge agreed; and, to his astonishment, she ripped up his driver's license.

Lorna was not afraid to admit when she was wrong. When she first came to the court she ruled that a woman whose husband had died should return some furniture for which the husband had not finished paying. "She later reversed her decision," reported the *Arizona Republic*, "because she discovered the law quite explicitly said the furniture should go to the widow." That taught Lorna something important.

"After that," she said, "I was a little more careful before I made a decision and if I wasn't sure, I'd take the case under advisement. I never had to change a decision again."

She was angry at the outcome of her first criminal case, which concerned the alleged rape of a four-year- old girl.

"The jury found the defendant not guilty and I was furious because to me he even looked guilty," she said. "That's one of the frustrations of being a judge—

watching a jury come back with a decision you don't agree with."

On the other hand, she was "badly shaken" the first time she passed the death sentence, "because I had to pronounce the end of an individual's life."

Lorna quickly became known as a strict judge, but she also knew when to temper justice with mercy. One ex-convict, who pleaded guilty to theft, told Judge Lockwood he had a wife and baby to support.

Lorna gave him probation, but warned him, "If you let me down you can expect the full penalty of five years in prison."

On another occasion, Lorna not only gave probation to a first offender who had stolen dishes and sheets for his girlfriend's apartment, but she also married the young couple before they left the courtroom!

Judges have the legal authority to marry couples, and Lorna seemed to enjoy providing that service. Describing one of the more unusual ceremonies she was asked to perform, she said, "A couple phoned me about ten o'clock one evening and said they wanted to be married immediately. The groom was in the army and had to leave within a day or two. I asked them if they had witnesses and they said 'yes.' Did they ever! A short time later, in they came with about a dozen friends and relatives. I had a very small apartment at the time and I was afraid the walls were going to bulge!"

One of the most important things Lorna did when she first became a judge was to make a permanent change in the setting for psychiatric hearings. She thought it was wrong for mentally ill people to be transported from the hospital, wait for hours at the courthouse, and then be forced to appear in a public courtroom. She got the law changed so that courtrooms were set up in hospitals, where people could attend their hearings in a quieter, less intimidating atmosphere. "I have a very strong feeling for the dignity of every individual," Lorna declared.

A year after Lorna became a judge, she was invited to Tucson by the American Association of University Women (AAUW) to speak to them on the topic of legislation, a subject with which she was, of course, very familiar. Lorna told the group that while she wanted to see more women in the state legislature, they need not be elected representatives to influence legislation. She urged them to request copies of bills from their legislators.

"You can get [them] for the asking," she advised. "Get to know your legislative and congressional representatives and let them know your opinions on legislation."

She then talked about bills currently before the legislature. "I am not advocating or opposing the adoption of these measures," she said, "but it is important that you keep informed on them."

Lorna told the group that the state school laws were "not really in good condition." She reminded them that the main purpose of their organization was "to advance education," and so they "should be interested in school law revisions." She was also concerned about the state of Arizona's adoption laws. She called them "uncertain in some respects and archaic." She urged the women to take a special interest in those outdated laws.

Lorna had an interest in adoption laws because, as a judge, she had to make decisions that would affect children for the rest of their lives. One memorable case came before her soon after she spoke to the AAUW. Her decision in that case revealed her unusual wisdom, as well as her ability to know exactly what to do in difficult situations.

"In 1952, I represented a young couple," recalled Walter Cheifetz, a lawyer with the firm of Lewis and Roca, "[who] wanted to adopt a three-year-old foster child who had been born to a woman who was not married. My clients had cared for this woman's little girl since birth. But, then, the birth mother died, and her sister, who had never before shown any interest in the child, came forward to claim her.

"As a young lawyer I was very adversarial, and I began to cross-examine the aunt in an antagonistic way. Suddenly, Judge Lockwood leaned over the bench. 'It's very nice of you, very unselfish of you, to come such a long distance from the East Coast,' Lorna said to the aunt. She then suggested we continue in her private chambers. When we were seated comfortably, Lorna once again talked to the aunt in a very gentle, kind voice. 'You've come all this way *now*,' she said. 'Why are you here *now*, when for three years your sister's child was with this other couple? Why *now*?' The aunt responded, 'The mother has died, and it is written in the scriptures that the

48

sins of the parents will be visited upon the children. It is my duty to take this child and punish it.'"

The young lawyer was horrified by the woman's statement, but Judge Lockwood's expression did not change.

"Well, it's so nice of you to take this interest," Lorna told the aunt politely.

The judge discovered exactly what she needed to know, and she did it by being respectful and courteous. She thanked everyone for attending. Later, she issued a written order that the child be adopted by the foster parents who had cared for her since birth.

"Well, that was an eye-opener to me," Walter Cheifetz said, "to see someone get at the truth by being nice. I learned that you can sometimes succeed with sugar and spice, and not by being a bulldog. Lorna so impressed me that I named my daughter after her!"

In 1953, Lorna's interest in the welfare of children and young people led her, finally, to the juvenile court, where, for three and a half years, she supervised sixty-one staff members and twenty probation officers.

As juvenile judge of Maricopa County, Lorna achieved statewide fame. She invited people from civic and church groups to observe her courtroom. She was sure, she said, that this would "result in helpful suggestions to the court." What she did not say was that this would enlighten the community as well. She wanted to make it clear that juvenile delinquency occurred in all classes of society.

"I've seen working, widowed mothers who have better plans for their children's welfare than others with time on their hands," she said.

Lorna's own upbringing in a very close and happy family influenced her beliefs. She said it was important that a "family had common interests," and that "without this closeness there is apt to be trouble." Lorna once visited a juvenile home where she encountered a young girl accompanied by one of her teachers. The girl was crying because she did not want to return to her own home.

"That instructor is probably the first adult that has ever been interested in the girl," Lorna said. "It's obvious the child is starved for love."

Her concern about children in whom no one was interested, or who might be at risk for other reasons, led Lorna to establish what would become one of her greatest legacies—the Arizona chapter of Big Brothers Big Sisters, the organization that matches adult mentors with children and young people.

Lorna believed people were responsible for their actions, but she did not think harsh retribution would make a difference in their lives. She did not believe in long sentences because "a long sentence merely embitters the person and he's likely to try it again. A shorter sentence establishes the idea that it's forbidden." Lorna's justice was quick and her sentences short. She became so famous that parents would sometimes threaten their children with her name.

"If you don't straighten out your life I'm going to send you to that Lorna Judge!" one woman told her teenaged daughter.

To the young people who appeared in her courtroom, Lorna gave advice which was often heeded. One such person, years later, sent Lorna a letter of thanks along with a picture of his wife and baby. She was occasionally stopped on the street by people who would say such things as, "You probably don't remember me, but thanks."

"What did I do for you?" Lorna would ask. "You did something *to* me," was the common reply, "but it changed my life."

Although Lorna was an outstanding juvenile judge, she said her work had given her "great emotional and mental strain, and caused her a lot of sleepless nights." In 1957, she resigned and returned to a regular courtroom.

As more young women entered the legal profession, Lorna gave them good advice.

"Be sure that you can be objective with others in the profession," she said, "and not be a 'woman lawyer'—just be yourself and a lawyer." She expected them to be competent. Virginia Hash remembered a woman who wanted to be a judge but, because Lorna did not think she had the capability to be on the bench, did not endorse her.

Lorna was extremely careful not to show favoritism to female lawyers in the courtroom. Elizabeth

Stover, who would one day become a Maricopa County Superior Court Judge, testified to that.

"She would encourage women attorneys," Stover said, "but she would not give them any special consideration."

She remembered that as a young lawyer, while waiting for her case to be called, she left the courtroom for a few moments to make an urgent phone call concerning another client.

"I went back to Judge Lockwood's court and [it] was completely empty except for the bailiff, who said 'Judge Lockwood would like to speak to you.' I had no idea what it was all about so I went back to her chambers and she proceeded to bawl me out for leaving her courtroom and not telling the bailiff where I was going. I apologized, but she let me know that just because I was a woman I couldn't get any special treatment."

They then returned to the courtroom for the hearing, which turned out well for Ms. Stover's client. When the judge left the courtroom, the bailiff approached Ms. Stover and told her that Judge Lockwood would like to see her again, briefly, in her chambers.

"I figured she'd probably cooled off a little bit and would tell me she didn't mean it quite that hard," Stover recalled. "Well! She proceeded to bawl me out a second time! I *never*, since that time, left a courtroom if I had a matter on the calendar without telling the bailiff where I was going. That shows that Judge Lockwood really did *not* give any special treatment to women.

"You had a lot of respect for her," Stover said. "You didn't disobey her. No one did. Not even the sheriff. Sheriff Cal Boise was powerful; he could be sheriff forever, if he wanted to be. But whenever Judge Lockwood wanted the sheriff to appear in her court, he dropped everything and appeared. She had red hair and you listened to what she said! But I don't recall her ever doing anything mean, even a slight hint of doing anything mean. She was a very bright, good person, interested in human beings, interested in doing justice to people."

Later, Ms. Stover represented a woman who had been arrested because, in a burst of hysteria, she grabbed a gun and shot and killed her husband's girlfriend. Despite the fact that the shooting did not appear to be premeditated, the woman was being tried for first degree

54

murder, which could carry the death penalty, instead of a lesser charge, which would entail a prison sentence.

"I liked the woman and I felt very sorry for her," Stover said. "She had gone really berserk, had just closed her eyes and pulled the trigger. On the fourth day of the trial Judge Lockwood let us know that she was not going to let the jury even consider first degree murder. So I was very relieved and I appreciated her doing that. I think it was the proper thing for her to do. I felt she was extremely learned in the law. She was a good judge, and she tried to rule the way the law was."

Attorney John Frank recalled that Lorna "was a great judge, maybe the best we've ever had. She was one of the great judges I've known in my life, and I've seen a lot of judges all over the United States." Frank, once a professor at Yale Law School, was one of the Arizona lawyers who participated in the defense of the *Miranda* case before the United States Supreme Court. The Supreme Court's *Miranda* decision requires police to advise a suspect of his rights: the right to remain silent; the right to an attorney; and, for those who cannot afford an attorney, a public defender.

"She was insightful, thorough, responsible," Frank said of Lorna. "She was firm. No one ever wasted time in her courtroom. We had only four or five judges back then, and if we had an especially hard case we tried to get it before Lorna Lockwood because she was the best. She ruled against me the first time I argued a case before her and she was absolutely right."

Frank remembered another case in which Lorna ruled in his favor. He called it "the Baby Ruth Candy Bar case." A woman bit into a Baby Ruth candy bar and broke her tooth on a piece of metal. The woman's dental bill to repair the tooth was $150, and that was all she wanted to get back.

"She wasn't a greedy lady," Mr. Frank said. He and his partner agreed to take the case and sue the candy company for the purpose of reforming the Arizona law.

"This was a major matter, a major problem in the state," he said. "It was a jurisdiction problem concerning when the citizens of Arizona could sue people in other states without actually going to those states. At that time you could not sue out of state for faulty products made in other states, and, of course, the Curtis Candy Company was in Illinois. So, we saw to it that we took this case before Lorna and she ruled in our favor. At the same time there was a similar case in Tucson which came out the other way. But the state supreme court upheld Lorna's rule, which reformed Arizona law.

"Judge Lockwood was prepared to be venturesome," Frank said. "She was not intimidated. She was the most progressive judge in the state."

"We all respected Lorna because she had a historical presence," stated Walter Cheifetz.

As Arizona's first woman judge, how easy it would have been for Lorna to rest on that bit of history! She need not have done more than that. She could have been overly cautious; she might never have questioned legal precedents; might have gone along with the way things had always been done; might have been more mindful of her reputation than of the effects of her decisions upon society. She could have played it safe. But that was not Lorna.

"I believe that duty and justice are the true measures of maturity of mind and security of conscience," she stated. In other words, to be an adult, to live with a clear conscience, means accepting responsibility, even when doing so is difficult. It means treating people fairly, even if they are not popular.

To the many lawyers who tried their cases before Judge Lockwood, she exemplified that maturity. "She was very fair," Elizabeth Stover later recalled, "a gracious lady."

"She seemed to me everything traditional integrity ought to be," John Frank said, "a great lady."

ᄋᎧ CHAPTER FOUR ᎧᏙ

Smooth Moves

As hard as Lorna worked, her life was not *all* work. She loved to read—especially history, historical novels, and detective stories. She loved her garden, where she grew not only flowers, but also the chives, mint, parsley, and dill she used in her cooking. She enjoyed giving dinner parties for her family and friends. Her specialties were Beef Stroganoff and angel food cake. Phoenix newspapers even printed her recipes in their food columns.

Through Lorna's political campaigns and her women's organizations she knew hundreds of people, and many had become her friends. One of those was, of course, Virginia Hash. Lorna liked to get away from work and "hide out" at Virginia's house (and in her swimming pool) on Saturdays, where it was "bedlam," according to Virginia, with "a football game going on [the] television" and the Metropolitan Opera broadcasting on the radio.

Lorna loved opera, and light opera, as well. She was very proud of her father's complete record collection of Gilbert and Sullivan's operettas. When in the late 1940s, Mesa High School began what would become a long tradition of presenting a Gilbert and Sullivan operetta each year, the students had no idea how they were supposed to sound and so needed to listen to recordings of professional performances. The choral director, Floyd Denton, who was also the assistant concert master of the Phoenix Symphony, had heard of Alfred Lockwood's collection. Although he had never met Lorna, she kindly offered to loan him the records when he called and explained his dilemma. Mr. Denton remembered going to the Lockwood house at 84 West Cypress.

60

"Judge Lockwood—although she wasn't a judge yet, she was still in the state legislature—was very gracious, very friendly," he said. "She was already quite well known. She said she recognized me from the symphony, which, of course, she attended regularly, but I think she was just being nice to say that. Her father, the retired chief justice, was there that day and he was very gracious, too…it was remarkable they were willing to lend me that record collection, because very few people in Phoenix had such a collection at the time, and the Lockwoods were quite rightly proud of theirs."

While adults often found Lorna somewhat intimidating, children rarely did. "She was everybody's aunt," said her friend and Chi Omega sister Stirley Cantor, who was one of the young lawyers Lorna encouraged in the Wednesday lunch group. "Lorna loved small children and they loved her." Stirley's own children adored Lorna. They loved to visit her and give her big hugs.

Although Lorna never married or had children of her own, she was devoted to her nine nieces and nephews.

"She took care of us a lot," Alan Cox said. "I think this added a realistic dimension to her life that she might not otherwise have had. Children do that. And when Lorna talked with you she was completely focused on you, no one else. She was never looking around for another dance partner! She was that way with everyone, children and adults."

"She went out of her way to be involved in our lives," Alfred Cox said. "She often bought us clothes, took us to the movies, and on vacations."

Lorna took them to California, to Catalina Island, and when they were older and could help with the driving, on cross-country trips to the East Coast. Her nephew, Chet Lockwood, lived with her while he attended Phoenix College. Years later, Lorna would say, "It would be difficult for me to live in a retirement community where there are no young people."

In 1960, after Lorna had served nearly ten years as a Maricopa County Superior Court Judge, she told her campaign manager, brother-in-law, and one-time law partner Simpson Cox that she would like to run for a seat on the Arizona Supreme Court. She said Justice Marlin T.

Phelps had told her that he wanted to step down from the bench and suggested that she run in the Democratic primary election to take his place. Simpson replied that he was willing to take on a new campaign, but on one condition.

"Aunt Lorna bristled," her nephew, Alan Cox, remembered. "She drew her well-endowed self up to her full five feet two inches. She reminded him that she never undertook anything with conditions attached. But, of course, she was curious to know what my dad's condition was. 'You must promise me,' he said, 'that when M.T. [Marlin T. Phelps] changes his mind and decides to run again, you won't withdraw your candidacy.' 'He won't change his mind,' Lorna said. 'Why would he?' 'Lorna,' Simpson said, 'I've known M.T. since we were seven years old. I know how his mind works. Just promise me.'"

Marlin Phelps did change his mind, just as Simpson predicted. Simpson Cox was a fierce campaigner from the time he was a student at Osborn Elementary school and rode his bicycle to the Phoenix City Council meeting, where he requested that the city set aside more parks for children to play in. The mayor told Simpson's father that children should be seen and not heard—advice

63

with which Simpson's father did not agree. Simpson's interest in city parks grew up with him; he became the lawyer responsible for Phoenix's mountain preserve laws.

Simpson successfully managed all of Lorna's campaigns. He always seemed to know when the time was right for her to run for office. He encouraged her to run for the state legislature in 1939, even though she thought she could not win. Simpson told her that she would win if she followed his advice.

"Don't declare your intention to run until the last minute," he said. "Your competitor will be going up to his cabin at Iron Springs outside of Prescott. *You* stay in Phoenix and campaign all summer while he's out of town."

Lorna followed Simpson's advice, and of course, won her first election, just as she won all that followed.

Lorna loved to campaign, but she had not always been a good public speaker. Virginia Hash recalled that in the beginning, Lorna was, in fact, a "terrible" speaker. Embarking on her own campaign to improve Lorna's public presentations, Virginia would sit in back of a room full of hundreds of people and listen to Lorna speak, then tell her everything she had done wrong. Lorna always wanted to know exactly how to improve.

"But, oh, she was great," Virginia said. "She learned. She became one heck of a fine speaker." Although a Republican, Virginia always supported Lorna because she "had a fine mind. If she hadn't been able I wouldn't have gone for her. She was plenty able." When Virginia went with Lorna to the State Democratic Convention in Yuma, where Lorna was speaking, Virginia wanted to know if she would get thrown out of the convention because she was a Republican.

"Just keep your mouth shut," Lorna said.

"Yes, ma'am, I will," Virginia promised.

Lorna spoke to diverse groups of people. She was unusual for a politician in the first half of the twentieth century in being able to address her constituency in two languages. Her undergraduate major in Spanish at the University of Arizona now became very useful. Depending on her audience, she sometimes spoke only Spanish, just as she did in the courtroom when necessary. In the latter instances, she made it clear that she always "rel[ied] on an interpreter for accuracy."

In addition to speaking Spanish fluently, Lorna had another advantage over her opponent; she had her own pilot. Virginia Hash flew Lorna all over the state during the 1960 campaign. Unable to be commissioned as a military pilot and fly combat missions because she was a woman, she had, as a civilian, flown transport for the Army to Hawaii and Canada during World War II. She was an excellent pilot. Sharing joint ownership of a plane with her brother, Virginia could fly Lorna anywhere in the state in about an hour.

Lorna was terrified the first time she flew in Virginia's "31 Charlie" Piper.

"Gingerly hoisting my tight skirt," she said, "I reached the foot rung, and bumbled into the seat beside Virginia. Then complete bafflement and bewilderment set in...the panel of gadgets, stops, pulls, buttons, dials, and gauges made my senses reel. The dashboard of a Chevy was never like this!" She did come to love flying, however. "I've survived many flights since then," Lorna said. "Though I haven't become a pilot, I do know the difference between an altimeter and a tachometer, and can proudly navigate a bit with aid of air maps and the topography."

Virginia recalled some "rare adventures" the two shared. When flying back from Northern Arizona on one occasion, the cloud cover prevented Virginia from seeing where they were going. The only thing she could pick up on the radio was station KTAR in Phoenix, which happened to be broadcasting Bizet's *Carmen*. Listening to the opera, Virginia used the signal to keep her course steady and zero in on Phoenix and Sky Harbor Airport.

During the 1960 campaign, Lorna was "furious" with her team because they had been late getting her posters out across the state. Virginia remembered that "[Lorna] was going to send them out by bus. I said, 'No...I know how to get them out faster. Let me get...my brother...I know he'll be glad to take [the posters].' Of course he was. He flew out with [Lorna] and she had these people waiting at these airports all over town, all over the state. He loaded that airplane up, it was just sagging...he said, 'I can't believe it. All these women out at these airports meeting us.' Her posters got up."

Virginia thought the posters were a "hideous" green color. "I know you like green," she told Lorna, "but *that* green, oh! Awful!"

The two were still arguing about the color when, later in the campaign, they flew from Safford to Globe. When they landed at the airport east of town Lorna "was still spurning about her…signs and I spotted some, and I got to laughing so durned hard I couldn't taxi the airplane. I had to stop it. She said 'What in the world are you laughing at?' All I could do was laugh and point. She saw what I saw, and the two of us sat there in the airplane and we just roared with laughter." Lorna's green signs had been put up in a prominent place—all around the outdoor toilet right in front of the runway. "You couldn't miss" them, Virginia said. "Those bilious green signs! We were advertised in Gila County. No doubt about it."

In the 1960 election, Lorna needed her base of support more than ever—those women's clubs which had always been crucial to her success. Below is an excerpt from a letter Lorna wrote during an earlier campaign to the Business and Professional Women's Club, for which she had held the offices of state president, western regional director, and national board chairman of public affairs. It illustrates how much Lorna counted upon the service organizations to which she had devoted so much of her life.

> *Time is getting very short, and I know that my opponent is campaigning vigorously, so I'm depending on Business and Professional Women's Club members for their much appreciated offer of help. Personal contact with friends and acquaintances on my behalf is very important, as I can't possibly meet all the voters.*
>
> *Cordially and gratefully,*
>
> *Lorna*

The Business and Professional Women always came through, as did the Soroptimists, the Arizona Federation of Women's Clubs, the Eastern Star, the American Association of University Women, and of course, her Chi Omega sisters from the U of A.

Lorna's nieces and nephews began, at an early age, to help Lorna in her campaigns. They recalled that Lorna was "fanatic" about campaign donations. She would accept no more than a certain amount of money from any law firm, whether it was composed of five people or fifty. She kept careful records of every single contribution and, after the election, remainders were returned to each donor depending upon the percentage of the particular contribution.

Alan Cox remembered his first campaign; the year was 1946 and he was three years old. Lorna told him, "the people who make rules for your mother and father and me are legisla*tors*. When they meet together they meet in the legisla*ture*. And to become a legislator I have to get people to vote for me in an election. I'd like you to go with me to meet some people and to ask them to vote for me." Alan took Lorna's hand and walked with her to a small apartment complex where she began knocking on doors. After listening to his aunt saying the same thing for the third time, Alan said he was tired and he wanted to go home.

"You'll have to hold up better than that if you want to be a politician!" Lorna joked.

As Alan grew older, he realized his presence was really a part of Lorna's plan; there were so many people she needed to talk to, and having him along made it easier for her to excuse herself and move on.

By 1960, when Lorna decided to run for the supreme court, Alan was in high school. Now he accompanied his aunt not just down the street but all over the state. Lorna, Alan, and Alan's cousin, Charlene

Lockwood, checked into a Flagstaff motel late one night after having been campaigning since six o'clock in the morning. In order to review their itinerary for the following day, they went to Lorna's room, where Lorna plopped down on the bed, sighed, and began pulling the hairpins out of her long red hair. There was a knock on the door. Lorna sprang from the bed and, within fifteen seconds, had redone her hair. Then, looking completely fresh with a smile in place, she opened the door to the motel manager.

"How may I help you?" she said.

"My wife is so embarrassed," the manager said, handing Lorna a potted plant. "We didn't recognize you when you arrived. We're so honored to have you here."

"Well, it's our honor to be your guests," Lorna replied smoothly.

She thanked him, closed the door, put the plant on a table, and then collapsed back on the bed where, for the second time, she began to pull the pins from her hair. Alan and Charlene burst into laughter.

"What?" Lorna said, looking up. "Why are you laughing?"

They only giggled louder at their aunt, lying in an exhausted heap. "Oh, I know why you're laughing," said Lorna. "But let me explain something. That man has as much right to my attention and consideration as if he were the only person I've talked with all day."

When they arrived in Prescott, Lorna insisted on campaigning on Whiskey Row. Leaving Alan and Charlene outside, she went into every saloon, walked up to the bartender, and said, "I'm Judge Lorna Lockwood from Phoenix, and I'm running for the supreme court. I'm asking for your support. May I put a poster in your window and leave some of my campaign literature with you?"

Stunned that such a well-known woman would walk into a bar in the middle of the day, every bartender promised Lorna his absolute support and placed a stack of her brochures next to the cash register.

Alan was worried that campaigning in saloons would make his Aunt Lorna look bad. He knew that Justice Marlin Phelps, who was now campaigning hard against Lorna, would never go into a bar! Lorna explained to her nephew that she could get away with it just because she was a woman. If she had been a man the bartender would have offered her a drink, which, of course, she would have had to refuse. But she was in and out of every saloon in sixty seconds, and the shock value, she said, was tremendous.

Lorna was acting on the advice she would one day give her law clerk, Roslyn Silver: "You'll always be underestimated [because you are a woman] and you should take advantage of that." In any event, Lorna had grown up in Douglas and Tombstone, two of Arizona's wildest frontier towns. Why would she be intimidated by Whiskey Row?

As Lorna, Charlene, and Alan walked along that day, they noticed a woman whose car door was stuck on the high curb. Alan approached the woman, asked if he could help, then lifted the door up and closed it. When the woman thanked him, he handed her a campaign brochure and said, "I'd like to introduce my aunt, Judge Lorna Lockwood, who is running for the supreme court."

"Smooth move," Lorna whispered.

The year 1960 was interesting in Arizona political history. On September 13, Rose Mofford, executive secretary to Secretary of State Wesley Bolin, published the registration of primary election voters which showed that, statewide, registered Democrats outnumbered registered Republicans more than two to one. Despite this, Republican Richard Nixon carried Arizona over the Democrat John F. Kennedy by ten points in the presidential election. The state supreme court election was another matter, however. No Republican was running; therefore, whoever won the Democratic primary would run unopposed in the general election. Winning the primary guaranteed the outcome of the election.

John Frank, the "Baby Ruth Candy Bar case" attorney, cheered Lorna on when she decided to challenge Marlin Phelps. Frank thought she was clearly the more highly qualified candidate. He had been one of her biggest supporters from the beginning. He remembered one very hot day in September at the end of the primary season. Lorna was making her final campaign rounds of Phoenix law firms and stopped by John's office at Lewis and Roca.

"She was exhausted when she got to my office," he said. "I had her take off her shoes and put her feet up." But half an hour later those feet hit the campaign trail again, and when the final votes were counted Lorna Lockwood had, once again, made history. Frank was delighted.

"This was a daring thing to do," he said, "to upset a sitting judge."

It was even more daring that a woman had done it. But that woman was not finished yet. She was on her way to the top.

ᴄᴌᴑ CHAPTER FIVE ᴄᴌᴑ

You've Come a Long Way, Baby

"Lady, you can't park there!" a security guard yelled at Lorna when she arrived at the Arizona State Capitol building to be sworn in on January 2, 1961, and parked her car in a space reserved for supreme court justices. Lorna convinced the guard otherwise. "It took some doing," she said, "but I finally persuaded him that I was entitled to it, even if I was a woman."

Despite that, it was a proud day for Lorna. She was the first woman ever to sit on the Arizona Supreme

Court. It was also a proud day for her family, who had now contributed two members to the highest court in the state. In the presence of the other four justices, her family, and her friends, Lorna put on the black robe of a supreme court justice. She was assisted by her nephew, Alfred Cox, who had just been admitted to the State Bar of Arizona. Shortly thereafter, Lorna entered her father's old office, suite 227, and sat down at the very desk he had used during his eighteen years of service on the court. She would now study his decisions in *Arizona Reports*, the bound volumes containing every Arizona Supreme Court decision ever made. "I cannot fill my father's shoes," she said. "I hope I can follow in his footsteps."

The Arizona State Supreme Court, which consists of five people, including the chief justice and the vice-chief justice, is now the higher of two appellate courts in Arizona. The lower appellate court, the court of appeals, was not established until 1965. So when Lorna first went to the supreme court in 1961, county superior court decisions were appealed directly to the supreme court.

People who bring lawsuits to court are called plaintiffs, as opposed to defendants, who are the targets of lawsuits. Plaintiffs and defendants unsatisfied with the

78

decision of the county superior court may appeal that decision to the court of appeals. In that court, the case is decided by three judges who review the documents from the lower court and hear the arguments of the lawyers, then vote to affirm the lower court's decision, reverse it, or remand (return) the case to the county court for a new trial. There are no trials in the court of appeals.

If the plaintiffs or defendants are still not satisfied, they may appeal the court of appeals' decision to the supreme court, which will then take one of two actions. The justices may refuse to review the case. In that event the decision of the lower court is final. Or the justices may agree to review the case. If so, they read the documents from the lower court and hear arguments from the lawyers for both sides. The five justices then review the decision of the lower court and, privately, vote to uphold it, reverse it, or return it to a trial court. After the vote, the chief justice assigns the case to one of the justices who will write the majority opinion, explaining why the lower court's decision was upheld or reversed.

Lorna would be responsible for writing nearly five hundred of those opinions over the next fourteen years. As a justice of the supreme court, Lorna's decisions now affected not only the citizens of Maricopa County but also those of the entire state of Arizona.

Mark Harrison, who had graduated from Harvard Law School the previous spring, was Lorna's first law clerk. Instead of having their own offices, the clerks shared the offices of the justices for whom they worked. Mark recalled that Lorna sat at her father's "great big desk," which had been in use since Arizona's territorial days, and that his own desk was right next to hers. Because he was always in the room, he heard all of her telephone conversations with judges and legislators, and learned a lot from that exposure. And Lorna gave him a lot of responsibility. His job was to draft the opinions about the cases which came before the supreme court for Lorna's consideration, revision, and approval. Mark said that Lorna "was not conscious of status." She was very democratic; she did not think she was better than other people.

Lorna loved to argue. She not only wanted to know what Mark thought about her opinions, but also wanted him to disagree with her. On one occasion, Lorna and Mark were arguing so loudly that someone, afraid for the justice's safety, knocked on the door to ask if everything was all right. Everything was perfectly fine, Lorna said, and after the door was closed, the two went right on shouting at each other. When Mark walked out of Lorna's office, a friend who had heard their loud voices asked him if he had been fired. Of course not, Mark said. Years later, he wrote in the *Arizona State Law Journal* that the "most important" thing about Lorna was her "open, inquiring mind."

Lorna loved "open, inquiring minds." She loved them so much that she wrote the court's unanimous ruling against the University of Arizona. When the university used various methods to prevent the *New Times* newspaper from being distributed on campus, Lorna reminded her beloved alma mater that the First Amendment to the United States Constitution guarantees freedom of speech and of the press. She quoted the U.S. Supreme Court decision in *Tinker v. Des Moines School District*: "In our system, students may not be regarded as closed-circuit recipients of only that which the state chooses to communicate. They may not be confined to the expression of those sentiments that are officially approved."

81

Lorna, of course, was not always in agreement with her fellow justices. She wrote the dissent in the *State v. Taylor* case, which came before the supreme court in 1975. A juvenile of low mental capabilities was suspected of setting a fire at the Pioneer Hotel in Tucson, which resulted in the deaths of twenty-eight people. He was arrested, brought to trial, and found guilty. The supreme court upheld the conviction. In dissenting from the majority, Lorna wrote that the police had not respected the juvenile's rights, nor had they followed proper procedure in detaining him at the police station. Although they had technically complied with *Miranda* in reading him his rights, he was not intelligent enough to know what that meant. He was questioned without being charged and without an attorney present. Although he changed his story throughout the seven continuous hours of interrogation, he never confessed to the crime. Lorna said that, ultimately, the boy had not been the recipient of "those constitutional principles guaranteed to all persons."

The American legal system is descended from and closely related to England's common law. Common law is that which judges make by applying common sense to solve issues between opposing parties. It is different from statutory law which is made by Congress, state legislatures, or by people voting in an initiative and referendum election, as may be done in Arizona.

Lorna knew a lot about the connection between American and English Common Law. Sometimes those old English laws were right, she said, and sometimes they were wrong. One law she thought was right was the Nuisance Law, which dates back to the sixteenth century when Queen Elizabeth I ruled England. When the Del Webb Corporation built the Sun City retirement community near the Spur Industries feedlots west of Phoenix, it knew very well those cattle lots would be a nuisance. But when the citizens complained about the smell and the health hazards, they were told by Spur that nothing could be done because the feedlots had been there first.

"Not so!" Lorna said. She invoked the Nuisance Law, which states that regardless of who was there first, the one causing the nuisance must move. But Lorna also said there must be a fair solution, so she ordered Del Webb to pay for the removal of the lots to another location.

On another occasion, Lorna thought English Common Law was wrong. A little over two years after she took her seat on the supreme court, she wrote the opinion in what most legal scholars consider her most important decision, *Stone v. Arizona Highway Commission*, commonly known as the sovereign immunity decision.

The sovereign immunity decision came about because of a terrible head-on collision that had occurred almost eight years earlier, on U.S. Highway 80 near Benson, east of Tucson. On September 27, 1955, a thirty-seven-year-old woman from Kentucky, Hathaway Stone, was killed and her husband Ernest and their two children, Darrell and Denise, were severely injured when their car collided with another vehicle. Hathaway, according to the medical report from Benson Hospital, died from "severe concussion" and "multiple fractures of pelvis and chest."

The collision occurred because the Arizona State Highway Department, after the completion of some road construction, failed to remove detour signs at the top of a hill where a new road intersected with an old one. Those signs, in fact, remained in place for several months after construction was finished.

Represented by the law firm of Udall and Udall in Tucson, Ernest Stone brought a lawsuit against the individual members of the Arizona State Highway Commission, the state engineers, and the construction company contracted by the state. Their carelessness, he charged, was responsible for the death of his wife and for the injuries to himself and his children. On May 7, 1959, Judge Raul H. Castro of the Pima County Superior Court in Tucson ruled against Mr. Stone. Judge Castro said that Mr. Stone was not allowed to sue the State of Arizona because of the rule of sovereign immunity.

Sovereign means supreme, and in English Common Law the sovereign was, of course, the king. *Immunity* means exemption or protection from any charge. Originating under King Henry IV, who ruled England from 1399–1413, sovereign immunity meant the king was not subject to the same laws as everyone else. In American law, it meant that citizens could not sue their own government.

On May 25th of that year, Ernest Stone appealed the superior court's decision to the Arizona Supreme Court, which handed down its decision four years later.

"Mr. Stone," Lorna wrote on April 25, 1963, "was misled by those markings into turning left into the path of an oncoming car which could not be seen as it was approaching from the east over the rise of the hill. The two vehicles collided, causing the death of Mrs. Stone and various injuries to Mr. Stone and the children."

Lorna believed the rule of sovereign immunity was outdated and irrelevant in the United States. She wrote that the concept had been "windblown across the Atlantic as were the pilgrims on the Mayflower and landed as if by chance on Plymouth Rock," where it became a "tumbleweed" traveling across America. She noted that "even though at a very early date in American history we overthrew the reign of the English king," we had not thrown out the rule which had originally been designed to protect him. And finally, she pointed out the ironic fact that the rule was no longer in effect even in England! "We are of the opinion," she wrote "that when the reason for a certain law no longer exists, the rule itself should be abandoned."

The supreme court's decision was mixed. While the State of Arizona could now be sued, the individuals who worked for it were protected. Lorna wrote that "it should be apparent that the State Highway Engineer could not personally be present at every place where construction or repair work on the highways of the state was to be performed."

And so the lower court's decision was "affirmed, in part, reversed in part." The supreme court sent the case back to the Pima County Superior Court where Judge Mary Ann Richey ordered that a new jury trial be set for September 14, 1966. The Stones won that trial, and on September 23 the jury awarded the Stones $68,000.

But in October of that year, Judge Richard Roylston denied the state's motion for a new trial. In November, the state's appeal was again denied, and yet again in 1968. Not until July 30, 1970, nearly fifteen years after the collision that had taken the life of their wife and mother and had left Ernest, Darrell, and Denise with disabilities did the State of Arizona pay the Stones $43,000—far less than the original 1966 judgment. Nevertheless, for the first time in its history the State of Arizona was allowed to be sued, and not only was it sued, but even after several appeals, it lost the lawsuit.

"There were very few lawsuits filed against the state prior to that decision," Lorna said, "because you had to receive permission from the state to sue. It was that old philosophy that the king can do no wrong." The *Phoenix Gazette* called *Stone v. Arizona Highway Commission* one of Lorna's "most controversial Supreme Court decisions."

Lorna was never afraid of controversy. "I have always prided myself in rendering decisions based on common sense, rather than strictly on legal precedent," she said years later. "I always have tried to do this and so has the Arizona Supreme Court." Lorna's "common sense" did indeed set legal precedent; her sovereign immunity decision was followed by similar rulings in much of the rest of the nation. She was the pioneer.

Lorna's pride in common sense influenced what she thought was her most important supreme court decision, *Shirley v. Superior Court.* Tom Shirley, a Navajo Indian, was elected to the Apache County Board of Supervisors in 1972. Although Mr. Shirley received the highest number of votes, his opponents tried to prevent him from taking his seat on the board, arguing that he was ineligible to hold public office because he lived on a reservation. According to Arizona law, they were right.

88

Although the State of Arizona had given Native Americans the right to vote in 1948, they were still restricted from full participation in Arizona politics. Shirley's opponents took their case to the Apache County Superior Court and won. When Mr. Shirley appealed that decision, he perhaps had no idea what an important step he was taking. Eventually his appeal made its way to the state supreme court where, in 1973, Lorna ruled in his favor. By reversing the lower court's decision Lorna did far more than make a judgment about the rights of one Native American; she changed the Arizona law for all Native Americans.

"In practicing what she preached," the *Arizona Weekly Gazette* later wrote, "Justice Lockwood ruled for the first time in state history that an Indian can't be barred from holding public office." Her nephew, Alan Cox agreed with Lorna's decision. She "did not tolerate the actions of people who discriminated on the basis of race, creed, or gender." Indeed, she did not. As Lorna had said on another occasion years before, "It's the right thing to do."

In 1965, Lorna did something no woman had done before. On January 11, the *Evening American* ran the headline, "New State Chief Justice Keeps Date With History." But this time Lorna's historical date was not only with the State of Arizona, but with all of America. When she was elected chief justice by her fellow supreme court justices, she became the first woman in the nation to head any state supreme court. Retiring Chief Justice Jesse Udall told the *Phoenix Gazette*, "This is the first time in the 189 years of our nation's history that the outstanding contributions of women in the judiciary...have been so recognized."

Senators, congressmen, and judges from all over the country congratulated Lorna the day she was sworn in. President Lyndon B. Johnson wrote, "I know that it must give you a great satisfaction to be the first woman selected as Chief Justice of a State Supreme Court. But it must be even more satisfying to know that your talent and legal ability have been recognized."

Lorna surely thought of her father that day, and of how, from the time she was ten years old, she had wanted to follow him. In an interview with ABC News, she declared, "This is just about the happiest day of my life."

As chief justice, Lorna was responsible for far more than the supreme court. "I supervise all judges in all the courts in the state," she told the *Evening American*, "and that's not an easy job." She was also in charge of setting up the lower court of appeals, the new intermediate court between the county superior courts and the supreme court. It was a lot of work, and she did it well. One of her fellow justices, Fred Struckmeyer, spoke of Lorna's "devoted and untiring efforts to make the court a great judicial body." In 1965, the chief justice of the Arizona Supreme Court served for one year. Lorna was elected to the position again in 1970. She became a powerful voice, not only in Arizona, but in legal circles throughout the United States.

The California chapter of the National Association of Women Lawyers (NAWL) launched a campaign for Lorna to be the first woman appointed to the United States Supreme Court. Their enthusiasm spread to other states. The NAWL was joined by all of Lorna's other organizations, who rallied to put her name forward. The idea was not new. When she was in Washington, D.C. in 1964 to attend the American Law Institute, her old friend John Frank invited her to a dinner at which she met all of the United States Supreme Court justices. In 1965 and again in 1967, Senator Carl Hayden of Arizona recommended Lorna to President Johnson.

When the president nominates someone for the supreme court, that nomination must be confirmed by the Senate. Senate confirmation is not an easy thing to achieve. There will always be senators who disagree with the nominee's position on various subjects or past judicial decisions. Because of this, the president tries to select a nominee who will garner enough votes to be confirmed. Although President Johnson was a strong supporter of women's rights, he perhaps did not think a female nominee could receive enough votes to be confirmed. In the 1960s, many people did not think women could do jobs as well as men; many thought, as did the governor of Arizona in the 1940s, that "no woman is capable of being a judge." (The more likely reason Johnson did not appoint a woman that year was because he believed he had a confirmable candidate in Thurgood Marshall, who would become the first African American on the supreme court. He was right.) When the president did not nominate Lorna, her supporters were disappointed. But Lorna, as always, was very gracious. "I like very much the work I am doing," she said. "That anyone would think I have the qualifications to serve on the United States Supreme Court is a great compliment."

Lorna remained committed to the women's organizations which had always supported her. In 1966, while running for a second term on the supreme court, she became president of the Phoenix Soroptimist Club. In 1968, she taught a non-partisan class in politics for women at the YMCA. In 1971, sponsored by the Business and Professional Women's Clubs, Lorna taught that same class throughout Arizona. She told women not only to help elect good people, but also to "seek public office" themselves. She wanted women to become every bit as involved in the political process as men.

The *Gardner v. Gardner* divorce case reveals Lorna's great concern about the rights of women. A man had been ordered by the superior court to pay alimony (living expenses) to his ex-wife, who did not work outside the home. As was true of most women of the time, she stayed home to cook, clean house, and raise their children. When the man decided to marry again, he no longer wanted to support his first wife. When the case came before the supreme court in 1964, Lorna ruled that the

93

man must continue to support his ex-wife. With one of her famous similes which made her point crystal clear, she wrote, "The obligations of a marriage cannot be thrown aside like an old coat when a more attractive style comes along."

Although Lorna once claimed not to be a militant feminist, she became more outspoken at the end of her career. In 1965, when she was elected chief justice, she stated, "I have found during all my professional life that most men make no distinction between professional men and women. They have accepted the fact that women in the professional field can do as well as men." But ten years later, when she retired from the supreme court, she apparently revealed what she truly thought. "I had to work twice as hard to be considered for those posts [judge, justice, chief justice] because I was a woman," she said.

Lorna strongly supported the Equal Rights Amendment (ERA), which states "Equality of rights under the law shall not be denied or abridged by the United States or by any state on account of sex." The amendment was written in 1923 by suffragist Alice Paul, in whose former home Lorna had lived when she worked in Washington, D. C. Beginning in 1923, the amendment was brought before every Congress, but it was not until 1972 that it finally passed. In order to become law, after an amendment to the U.S. Constitution is passed by Congress, it must then be ratified by three-fourths (thirty-eight) of the fifty states. Only thirty-five states ratified the ERA, on which Congress set a seven-year time limit for ratification; Arizona was not among them, and Lorna was not happy about that. She was "an indefatigable campaigner for the ERA," said Judge Mary Schroeder, "and she was scheduled to lead a rally in support of the amendment at the state Capitol. She took the podium and announced that because the ERA had become so politicized—*so politicized!*—and because judges are not supposed to be political, she would have nothing to say about it. Then Lorna introduced a speaker who gave a rousing ERA speech. So, in announcing she would not lead the rally, Lorna, in effect, led it."

Lorna called those who opposed the ERA "brainwashed." She had always said that people who made up their minds about any situation before they knew the facts were "downright damaging," She clearly explained her position on the ERA.

I can't understand why some women are against it...Their ideas seem to have been fed to them. Some of their objections are frivolous, such as one woman here who insisted women would lose separate toilets. What about airliners? I've never seen separate toilets on an airplane, and haven't heard any objection. Others claim women will be drafted if ERA would be passed. I see no objection to that. Women could be drafted, at any event, if the Congress wanted to, tomorrow, and in any capacity. There's nothing in the Constitution that forbids it, and it was almost done in World War II. The ERA doesn't attempt to make a change between feminine and masculine, but in legal points only...It is part of the onward march for equalization in the legal sense, just as achieving voting rights...There were awful prophecies then, too, about what would happen if women were allowed to vote; I don't think there has been much difference in government because of women's suffrage. It seems to me it is older men who fear this change, who feel threatened. Young men don't.

Her secretary reported that Lorna's "red hair glows when she is angered." When Lorna defended the ERA her hair must have been flaming. That red hair. For

96

years the lawyers called her Goldilocks because of that hair. "Well, Goldilocks just handed down this decision," they would say, or "You know what Goldilocks thinks about that." She seemed not to mind. She always said you had better have a "good sense of humor" if you wanted to be in the legal profession.

In 1974, the year before Lorna retired from public office, the people of Arizona voted to amend the Arizona Constitution to provide for the merit appointment of judges. The amendment was the result of Maricopa County Superior Court Judge Thomas Tang's re-election loss following his refusal to try two teenagers as adults. Although the state supreme court upheld Tang's ruling and he was highly respected within the legal community, his decision became so unpopular with the public that he was voted out of office. (In 1977 he was appointed to the U.S. Court of Appeals for the Ninth Circuit, where he served for eighteen years.) For this reason judges are now appointed by the governor upon the recommendation of a nominating commission. The commission is made up of members of the Arizona State Bar Association as well as non-lawyers, and is bipartisan, consisting of both Republicans and Democrats. The merit appointment system applies to superior court judges in counties with populations of 150,000 or more. It also applies to all appellate court judges and supreme court justices. This important amendment makes the judiciary, for the most part, independent of any political party. Judges are appointed for their ability, not elected because of their popularity.

Lorna, of course, had had no choice but to run as a political candidate. Later, she admitted that it had been easier to run for the state legislature. "It was easier for women to go into politics in those days [in the legislature]," she said. "The general public felt anyone could go into politics. They didn't feel that way about the law. They thought that takes some brains."

By 1975, Lorna had been on the supreme court for fourteen years, had been a Maricopa County Superior Court judge for ten years before that, served three terms in the state legislature, worked in Arizona's Congressional office in Washington, D.C., and been assistant attorney general for two years. She had served her state well. But now she was seventy-two years old, battling diabetes and high blood pressure, and had suffered a small stroke. On May 15th, to the sorrow of her fellow justices and friends, she held a press conference at the supreme court to announce that in September she would retire. She spoke with her usual dignity and smiled at the television cameras. Later, when interviewed by a reporter from the *Arizona Republic,* she was much less formal. "I did my durndest," she said, sounding like the girl from Tombstone.

"Justice Lorna Lockwood...challenged traditions with knowledge," wrote the *Phoenix Gazette,* and "made her way with grace and beauty to high places in what was undeniably a man's world."

The *Arizona Republic* was equally laudatory. "Justice Lockwood's chief contribution to the bench was a creative mind. In a profession bound by precedent, she was unafraid of new concepts that could contribute to the administration of justice."

On September 21st, six days after Lorna hung up her black robe for the last time, her friends honored her with a banquet in the grand ballroom of the Adams Hotel in Phoenix. According to the *Mesa Tribune,* "More than 900 persons from across the state and county gathered to pay tribute." In fact, there were twice that many people, far more than the Phoenix Fire Code allowed for that room. Even after the banquet was sold out, people tried to get tickets, including a former Democratic governor. "Too bad," said Virginia Hash, who had organized the event. "He should have called earlier." Lorna told her Republican friend that she'd better get the governor tickets—or else. "Or else what?" Virginia asked. "Or else I won't show up myself," Lorna retorted.

When Lorna, escorted by her family, entered the ballroom and saw some two thousand people gathered there, she suddenly stopped and stared in amazement. For the first time in her life she appeared to be speechless. She listened to all of the tributes, to the letters from President Gerald Ford and United States Supreme Court Chief Justice Warren Burger. But the thing she loved the most was a giant life-sized poster of herself as a toddler in Douglas. In the photograph she looks right into the camera and her right hand is lifted in a judicial gesture. Around the poster her friends had inscribed the words, "You've Come a Long Way, Baby."

Lorna joined her brother-in-law Simpson Cox and her nephew Alfred in the law firm of Cox and Cox, located on the third floor of the Luhrs Tower, where she and Loretta Savage had set up their practice thirty-six years before. In contrast to that earlier time, there was now plenty of work if Lorna wanted it, but she elected to be "of counsel" and keep irregular office hours. Simpson's brother, who was also a member of the firm, said they should put a sofa in Lorna's office so she could take a nap whenever she wanted. He said she had earned it.

In April of 1977, on Maundy Thursday, Lorna attended a service at First Congregational Church in Phoenix. After the service, as she walked across the parking lot to her car, she tripped and fell, breaking her jaw, her arm, and her shoulder. An ambulance took Lorna to Good Samaritan Hospital. Her family was not notified for four hours. When Lorna's sister Charlotte finally arrived, she found Lorna in a hospital bed in a hallway. She had not yet been seen by a physician. Lorna never recovered from that fall. She was in and out of the hospital for the next five months. On September 23rd, 1977, she died of pneumonia at Good Samaritan Hospital at age seventy four.

On September 27, there were two memorial services for Lorna—one at her church and the other in the rotunda of the state Capitol. Lorna's nephews, Alfred and Alan, remembered the funeral of Lorna's father, their grandfather, Chief Justice Alfred Lockwood, which had also been held in the Capitol rotunda. They were children then, and recalled standing on the balcony looking down at their grandfather's casket, far beneath the dome and atop the mosaic of the Arizona star on the floor. Lorna's service was in the same place as her father's, but there was no casket; in her will she had written, in her own hand, that she would be cremated.

At the Capitol that morning Governor Raul Castro spoke, as did five others: Chief Justice Duke Cameron, Vice Chief Justice Fred Struckmeyer, State Representative Polly Rosenbaum, Judge Warren McCarthy, and Lorna's dear old friend, Virginia Hash. Lorna's pastor, Hugh Shelby Lee, pronounced the benediction.

"Lorna was destined for a legal career from birth," wrote the *Arizona Republic*. "Her father, Alfred C. Lockwood, was a giant of the state judiciary, reaching (as his daughter did later) the post of chief justice. She was hearing about legal briefs when most Arizona girls were playing jacks."

When Lorna was hearing those legal briefs more than sixty-five years earlier in the southeastern Arizona Territory, she knew exactly what she wanted to do when she grew up. And, somehow, against all odds, she did it.

☙ CHAPTER SIX ❧

Lorna's Legacy

A Barbie doll dressed in a black judicial robe stands on a mahogany pedestal covered with brass plaques engraved with the names of nine women judges: Mary M. Schroeder, Sarah D. Grant, Elizabeth Stover, Marilyn Riddle, Dorothy Carson, Alice Truman, Lillian S. Fisher, Mary Ann Richey, and Sandra Day O'Connor. The doll, called the Lorna Lockwood Memorial Traveling Trophy, was retired and given to the Arizona Historical Society in Tempe by Justice Sandra Day O'Connor when she was appointed to the United States Supreme Court.

105

The trophy was the idea of two judges, Mary
Schroeder and Sarah Grant, both mothers of young girls.
They decided it would be fun to take Barbie out of her
bikini and make her a judge. Judge Barbie would certainly
be a better role model for their daughters than Bikini
Barbie! Schroeder recalled the doll's history, and how the
joke turned into a tradition. "Sarah presented it to me, and
then I presented it back to her, and we decided to keep on
presenting it to other women judges until an Arizona
woman was appointed to the United States Supreme
Court. Of course, we thought that would take fifty years,
and we were stunned when a couple of years later Sandra
Day O'Connor was appointed. So Sandra O'Connor took
Judge Barbie with her to Washington, D.C. and then she
gave it to the historical society."

Judge Barbie, which began as a joke, now stands
as an honored symbol of Lorna Lockwood's pioneering
spirit. "The history of women judges in Arizona is a
powerful story," said Schroeder, who was a beneficiary of
that spirit. She first met Lorna in 1970, when she clerked
for Justice Jesse Udall and Lorna was serving her second
term as chief justice. Lorna invited Schroeder to a
Soroptimist Club meeting, and she became a lifelong

member. In 1975, Lorna, who was adamant that women serve on the appellate courts, influenced Schroeder's appointment by Governor Castro to the Arizona Court of Appeals, the first such appointment under Arizona's new merit system. "She did not want to leave the appellate courts without women," Schroeder said. "Arizona has had so many women judges on the appellate courts, and all because of Lorna. I believe Arizona has had more women chief justices on a state supreme court than any other state...and all because of Lorna.

"I was so proud," Schroeder said, "when I introduced my mother to Lorna Lockwood at the reception following my appointment to the state court of appeals. When Lorna described me as her protégée, I was so proud. I had always thought of Lorna as my mentor but I didn't know if she considered herself that, so when she called me her protégée, I was so proud."

Five years later, Schroeder was appointed by President Jimmy Carter to the United States Court of Appeals for the Ninth Circuit in San Francisco. The Ninth Circuit hears appeals of U.S. District Court decisions from Alaska, Arizona, California, Hawaii, Idaho, Montana, Nevada, Oregon, and Washington. In 2000, after twenty years on the Ninth Circuit, Mary Schroeder became its chief judge. Lorna would have been delighted by her protégée's success.

Schroeder did not exaggerate when she described Arizona women in the judiciary as a powerful story. At this time, six women, including Chief Judge Ann A. Scott Timmer, serve on the Arizona Court of Appeals. Although only two women have come on the Arizona Supreme Court since Lorna Lockwood, both of them, Ruth V. McGregor and Rebecca White Berch, have held the office of chief justice. Of the seventeen federal judges for the United States District Court for Arizona, five of them are women, including Susan Bolton, a later member of Lorna's Soroptimist Club, and Chief Judge Roslyn O. Silver, who began her own career clerking for Lorna on the supreme court.

In contrast to Arizona's history, the state of New York did not have a woman on a higher court until Judith S. Kaye was appointed to the court of appeals in 1983, twenty-three years after Lorna was elected to the Arizona Supreme Court. In 1967, *The American Biographical Encyclopedia* recorded that "only three female Supreme Court Justices are now serving in all the fifty states."

"Civilization is based upon law and order and the sense of permanency they provide," Lorna once said. "A democratic society is different from a dictatorship in that sense of permanency." And, of course, in the sense of equality. Lorna's first law clerk, Mark Harrison, wrote that "Justice Lockwood has always been regarded as an articulate leader in the struggle for equality under the law."

Equality under the law is symbolized by Lady Justice. Statues of Lady Justice are present in courts of law from London to Tokyo to Washington, D.C., and have been around in one form or another since antiquity. She was the goddess Maat in ancient Egypt; the goddess Themis in Greece; and the goddess Justitia in Rome. The modern Lady Justice holds scales in one hand and a sword in the other. With the scales Lady Justice weighs both sides of the case before her; with the sword she dispenses justice. While she weighs the scales and wields the sword, she must be impartial. To show her impartiality she often wears a blindfold. She must not consider the color of a person's skin, or whether the person is rich, poor, male or female. Equality under the law.

Equality under the law? Not everywhere, of course. In spite of the statue of a woman which adorns the United States Supreme Court, its inhabitants were, until 1981, only men.

Then everything changed. On September 25th, President Ronald Reagan named Judge Sandra Day O'Connor from the Arizona Court of Appeals to be the first woman on the United States Supreme Court.

John Frank said that Lorna "was the snowplow that broke the path for women in this state." And perhaps beyond. Lorna influenced legal circles throughout the nation. When, in 1970, the American Trial Lawyers Association honored Lorna with its annual Award of Merit they described her well. "Writer of Many...Beautifully Wrought Opinions teaching the profound truth that the mission of the law is to accommodate change within a framework of continuity and to this end judges should not sit like the figure on the silver coin, ever looking backward." Lorna, of course, was famous for never looking backward.

In the end, Justice O'Connor said it best. "Each position I held in Arizona was one which was attained by following a course made far more accessible because Lorna Lockwood had prepared the way by proving it could be done and done well by a woman.

"Today my chambers window in Washington, D.C. commands a view of a red brick house, the headquarters of the National Woman's Party and the former home of suffragist Alice Paul. It is also the very house which in the 1940s provided lodging to Lorna Lockwood when she served as administrative aide to Congressman John Murdock. As I look out my window each day, I am reminded of the contributions Lorna Lockwood made in opening doors for other women in the legal profession. Her kindly interest and encouragement of other women lives on in the work of those of us who were privileged to know her."

Lorna Lockwood's "kindly interest and encouragement" brought many women to heights they might not previously have thought possible, from women who ascended to the highest courts in the land to the five Girl Scouts who grew up to be lawyers because they once visited the Arizona Supreme Court and the chief justice encouraged them to consider the law as a career.

Lorna's legacy never ends. Whenever a woman tries a case or presides over a courtroom or writes a landmark decision, Lorna's legacy lives on.

∽ LORNA'S AWARDS ∾

- University of Arizona Medallion of Merit, 1960

- University of Arizona Alumni Achievement Award, 1961

- Award of Merit, Arizona Conference on Crime and Delinquency Prevention and Control, 1961

- Woman of the Year, State Federation of Business and Professional Women's Clubs, 1962

- Woman of Distinction Citation, Pacific Region of Soroptimists, 1962

- Humanitarian Award, Southern Pacific Region of Hadassah, 1965

- Woman of the Year, Kansas City Advertising and Sales Executive Club, 1965

- Woman of Achievement Award, American Association of University Women, Phoenix, 1966

- Outstanding Woman in the Field of Law Citation, *Who's Who of American Women*, 1967

- Woman of Achievement, Arizona, Association for Women's Active Return to Education, 1968

- Award of Merit, American Trial Lawyers Association, 1970

- Law and Government Award, Builder of a Greater Arizona, 1971

- Brotherhood Award, National Conference of Christians and Jews, 1972

- University of Arizona Alumni Distinguished Citizen Award, 1972

- Arizona Fifth District of the American Legion "Americanism Award," 1973

- Woman of the Year, Phoenix Advertising Club, 1974

- Very Outstanding Phoenician Award, City of Phoenix, 1975

- One Hundred Women and Minority Lawyers Award, Maricopa County Bar and State Bar of Arizona, 2000

◈ *PHOTOGRAPHS* ◈

1. Baby Portrait of Lorna, Douglas, Arizona Territory, 1903. Source: Alan Cox

2. Lorna with her uncle, Chester Lincoln, Douglas, circa 1905. Source: Alan Cox

3. Daisy holding Lorna in front of the Lockwood house, Douglas, circa 1905. Source: Alan Cox

LORNA LOCKWOOD MASCOT OF DOUGLAS HOSE CART TEAM

4. Lorna as mascot to Douglas hose cart team, circa 1908.
Source: Alan Cox

5. The Lockwood family in Tombstone. L to R: Lorna, Daisy, Judge Lockwood. Chester and Charlotte are in the front. Source: The Cox family

6. Lorna wearing Chi Omega Sorority pin, University of Arizona. Source: Alan Cox

THE·VNIVERSITY·OF·ARIZONA·

GREETING·
·TO·ALL·TO·WHOM·THESE·LETTERS·SHALL·COME·

THE·BOARD·OF·REGENTS·OF·THE·VNIVERSITY·OF·ARIZONA
BY·VIRTVE·OF·THE·AVTHORITY·VESTED·IN·IT·BY·LAW·AND·ON·THE·REC:
OMMENDATION·OF·THE·VNIVERSITY·FACVLTY·DOES·HEREBY·CONFER·ON·

LORNA·E·LOCKWOOD

WHO·HAS·SATISFACTORILY·COMPLETED·THE·STVDIES·PRESCRIBED·THEREFOR·
THE·DEGREE·OF·

JVRIS·DOCTOR

WITH·ALL·THE·RIGHTS·PRIVILEGES·AND·HONORS·THEREVNTO·APPERTAINING·
IN·WITNESS·WHEREOF·THE·SEAL·OF·THE·VNIVERSITY·IS·HERETO·AFFIXED
DONE·AT·TVCSON·ARIZONA·THIS· THIRD DAY·OF· JVNE
·IN·THE·YEAR·OF·OVR·LORD·ONE·THOVSAND·NINE·HVNDRED·AND·TWENTY· FIVE

7. Lorna's original law degree from the University of Arizona, 1925. Source: Alan Cox.

8. Alfred C. Lockwood, Chief Justice of the Arizona
Supreme Court. Photograph by Thomas Henry Bate,
1930. Arizona State Library, Archives, and Public
Records, Archives Division, Phoenix, #01-9438.jpg

9. Original campaign poster for the 15th Legislature, 1947. Source: The Cox Family

10. Lorna when she was a member of the 18th Legislature, 1947. Photograph by Thomas Henry Bate. Source: The Cox Family

11. The Superior Court Judges of Maricopa County, circa 1955. Source: Alan Cox

12. Judge Lockwood presiding at an adoption hearing, Superior Court in Maricopa County, circa 1954. Source: Arizona Photographic Associates, Inc., #69339

13. New member of the Arizona Bar, Alfred Cox, assisting his Aunt Lorna with her robe before she is sworn onto the Arizona Supreme Court, January, 1961. Justice Renz Jennings is pictured at right. Source: Alfred Cox

14. The five justices of the Arizona Supreme Court, circa 1962. L to R: Renz L. Jennings, Jesse A. Udall, Charles C. Bernstein, Fred C. Struckmeyer Jr., Lorna Lockwood. Source: Alan Cox

15. Lorna Lockwood, the first woman in America to become a chief justice of any state supreme court, 1965. Source: Alan Cox

16. Official portrait of Lorna Lockwood, Chief Justice of
the Arizona Supreme Court. Source: Arizona State
Library, Archives, and Public Records, Archives
Division, Phoenix, #97-7013.jpeg

17. The national convention of Business and Professional
Women, Miami Beach. Lorna is seated third from right.
Source: Alan Cox

131

18. Lorna Lockwood, Woman of the Year, Business and
Professional Women, 1962. Source: Alan Cox

19. Chief Justice Lorna Lockwood with five of her law
clerks, L to R; John Hough, George Hilty, Richard
Skousen, Lorna; Richard Mallery, Mark Harrison

20. "You've Come A Long Way, Baby" poster presented to Lorna upon her retirement from the Arizona Supreme Court. Source: Alfred Cox. Photograph of poster by Ron David Studio, Chandler, 2001

21. The Lorna Lockwood Traveling Memorial Trophy (Judge Barbie) was to be passed on from one woman to another until one of them was appointed to the United States Supreme Court. Arizona Historical Society's Museum at Papago Park, Tempe. Photographed by Richard David with permission of the museum staff

22. When Sandra Day O'Connor was appointed to the United States Supreme Court, she was given the Lorna Lockwood Trophy which she took to Washington D. C. before presenting it to the Museum at Papago Park. The trophy is now on display in the Sandra Day O'Connor exhibit in the museum. Photographed by Richard David with permission of the museum staff.

136

ACKNOWLEDGMENTS

I am grateful to the people who generously shared with me their memories of Lorna Lockwood: Lorna's late sister, Charlotte Lockwood Cox; Lorna's nephew, attorney Alfred Cox; Lorna's first law clerk, Mark Harrison of Osborn Maledon; the late Edward Jacobson of Snell and Wilmer; the late John Frank of Lewis and Roca; Lyman Manser, also of Lewis and Roca, who introduced me to John Frank; Walter Cheifetz of Lewis and Roca; the Hon. Elizabeth Stover, retired, of the Maricopa County Superior Court; the Hon. Mary Schroeder, U.S. Court of Appeals for the Ninth Circuit; and the Hon. Rose Mofford, former governor of Arizona, who provided me with many important clippings, as well

137

as a copy of the leaflet distributed at Lorna's memorial service at the Capitol. My special thanks to Melanie Sturgeon and Wendi Goen of the Arizona State Archives; to Astrid Norvelle of the Law Library at the University of Arizona; and to Lisa Patton of Legal Records of Pima County.

I owe an incomparable debt to Lorna's nephew, Alan Cox, who, on many occasions over a period of ten years, told me wonderful stories of his aunt, and on drives around Phoenix, showed me where those stories had taken place.

I am especially grateful to Eddie Basha, who introduced me to Lorna's family.

My thanks go, most of all, to my husband, Richard, who called me one day from the county court house in Phoenix, told me he was in the jury room named after Lorna Lockwood, and said "Why don't you write about her?" And then made certain I did.

~SWD
December 16, 2011

SONJA WHITE DAVID

ABOUT THE AUTHOR

At the age of ten Sonja David wrote a play based upon the Book of Ruth for her youth group to perform for the Wednesday night pot-luck supper at the church.

At the age of twelve she wrote a weekly column about her junior high school for the town newspaper, the Chandler Arizonan.

When she was seventeen she edited the school literary magazine, the Desert Breeze. After she attended the Bennington College Summer Writer's Workshop in Vermont where she studied under Alan Cheuse, author and book reviewer for National Public Radio's All Things Considered, she wrote book reviews for the Denver Post and feature articles for Bloomsbury Review and Denver Magazine. Lady Law is her first book.

Sonja lives on the Arizona desert with her husband, Richard, her granddaughter, Jennie Jane, and her black Bombay cat, Sheba. She is currently at work on a memoir about her five years on the San Carlos Apache Reservation.

SOURCE NOTES

Introduction

- *In the mid-1940s, a delegation:* Interview, Alan Cox.
- *"One of her favorite words":* Ibid.

Chapter One: Pioneer Girl

- *expected, at any moment, the birth of their first child:* Interviews, Alfred Cox and Alan Cox.

- *Alfred Lockwood was born in Ottowa, Illinois:* Ibid.

- *That same year he sent for his mother:* Ibid.

- *Lorna's mother, Daisy Lincoln:* Ibid.; Nancy Matte and Thomas Jacobs, "Justice Was a Lady: A

Biography of the Public Life of Lorna E. Lockwood"
(unpublished manuscript, 1985); 4–5.

- *a Canadian mining engineer, James S. Douglas:* Jane
Eppinga in Barry Gartell, ed., *Times Past: Reflections
from Arizona History* (Phoenix, AZ: Arizona Capitol
Times, 2008), 138, 146.

- *Captain Tom Rynning brought in:* "Douglas Station,"
U.S. Customs and Border Protection website.

- *Alfred referred to their first home:* Interview, Coxes.

- *Three years earlier, because of:* "Haunts and
History," "The Last of the Grand Hotels,"
hotelgadsden.com,

- *the revolutionary soldiers of Francisco Madero
defeated the federal troops of the dictator Porfirio
Diaz:* Lynn Davies, *History of the Mexican
Revolution,*
www.ic.arizona.edu/ic/mcbride/ws200/mex-davi.htm.

- *Lorna and her father were among those:* Interview,
Edward (Bud) Jacobson; also in the Cox interviews.

- *She was influenced by:* David Quantz, "Lorna
Lockwood: A Dynamic Woman in Changing Times"
(unpublished manuscript, 1986), 1.

- *"soft-spoken and gentle, but very strong-willed":*
Alfred Lockwood, quoted by Alan Cox in interview.

- *A few weeks before her death:* Eulogy given by the
Rev. Dr. M. Dosia Carlson at Charlotte Cox's
memorial service, Church of the Beatitudes, Phoenix,
AZ, December 6, 2003.

- *Lorna was eight years old when she enrolled:* Quantz, 1–2.

- *Daisy Lockwood made certain:* Interview, Charlotte Cox.

- *"I thought it would be wonderful to be a lawyer":* Henry Kiel, "Arizona's Chief Supreme Court Justice," *Arizona Days and Ways Magazine* 25 (April1965), 6.

- *"As I watched Dad I wished more than ever":* "Lorna E. Lockwood Heading for Bench, Is About To Realize A Lifelong Ambition," *Phoenix (AZ) Gazette,* September 13, 1950, first edition.

- *gave women the right to vote:* Jeff Malatin, *II: Women in Arizona Politics: From Suffrage to Governing,* Arizona Women and Politics, http://www.ic.arizona.edu/ic/mcbride/ws200/pol.htm.

- *Sarah Herring Sorin, the first woman:* Eppinga and Kasper in Gartell, 198.

- *Tombstone was a frontier town:* "Tombstone, Arizona," *The City of Tombstone's Official Website,* http://www.cityoftombstone.com.

- *Ed Schieffelin struck silver:* Edward Peplow, Jr., *History of Arizona, Vol.II* (New York: Lewis Historical Publishing Co. Inc., 1958), 195–6.

- *the famous Bird Cage Theater:* This Month in History, *Arizona Highways,* December 2008.

- *"the toughest town in the nation":* Edward Peplow, Jr., *History of Arizona, Vol.I* (New York: Lewis Historical Publishing Co. Inc., 1958), 616.

- *"14 murders and assassinations in 10 days.":* Eppinga in Gartell, 192.

- *On February 25, 1881, in a fight:* Ibid., 94.

- *There was much violence:* S.J. Reidhead, "Life in 1881 Tombstone, Arizona (blog entry)," *Blogcritics Culture,* last modified October 8, 2006, http://blogcritics.org/culture/article/life-in-1881-tombstone-arizona.

- *"it is difficult to decide who among them was good":* Peplow, vol. II, 613

- *"a horse thief, a robber, and an outlaw":* Old Tombstone, http://www.discoveraz.com/History/TStonehtml

- In 1886, the mines filled with water": "On This Date in Arizona History," Arizona Republic, May 12, 2012.

- "the secretary of the Arizona livestock board": "On This Date in Arizona History," *Arizona Republic,* May 23, 2011.

- *The Lockwoods lived across the street:* Matte and Jacobs, 5.

- *Water had to be pumped:* Told to the author by her grandmother, Nettie Denton, born in 1864.

- *when Lorna was thirteen years old:* Quantz, 2.

- *Alfred and Daisy not only encouraged:* Interview, Alan Cox.

- *lively discussions at the dinner table:* Quantz, 2.

- *Charlotte recalled how one:* Interview, Alan Cox.

- *When Lorna attended Tombstone High School:* Matte and Jacobs, 6.

- *Lorna took an important step:* Sonja White David, "Lady Law: The Legacy of Lorna Lockwood," *The Eleusis of Chi Omega* (Fall 2001), 46–47.

- *she first decided she would one day run:* Jean Duffy, "Law Was Her Career Ever Since Age of 10," *Arizona Republic* (Phoenix, AZ), September 8, 1966.

- *what she called her "base of support":* Interview, Alan Cox.

- *Lorna was front-page news:* "Tombstone Girl Honor Candidate of Phi Kappa Phi," *Tombstone (AZ) Epitaph*, April 1, 1923.

- *"Law school is no place for a woman":* Matte and Jacobs, 1.

- *"the dean did everything he could to dissuade me":* "Retired Justice Lockwood Says She Favors ERA," *Phoenix Gazette*, September 18, 1975.

- *He thought she should become a secretary:* Interview, Alan Cox.

- *"So I went into the law school":* Matte and Jacobs, 6–7

- *Lorna may have been shy:* Matte and Jacobs, 6–9

- *It was assumed that should a woman:* Interview, Mary Schroeder.

- *there were some things:* Matte and Jacobs, 19.

- *Although she was the second woman:* Quantz, 2.

- *the only member of her class:* E-mail interviews, Astrid Norvelle.

- *Dean Fegtly complimented Lorna:* Quantz, 2.

- *"I think he was proud of me":* Phil Andrews, "Decisions of Wisdom," Lockwood Behest, *Arizona Weekly Gazette* (Phoenix, AZ), October 4, 1977.

- *university president Richard Harvill wrote:* Cox Family collection.

Chapter Two: Lady-in-Waiting

- *"My original plan":* Matte and Jacobs, 10.

- *"fortuitous, not planned in definite steps. ":* Duffy.

- *as her father's secretary and law clerk:* Virginia Hash, Interview for the Evo De Concini Oral History Project. *Arizona Legal History Project.* Arizona Historical Society Library and Archives, Central Arizona Division, Tucson, AZ.

- *She found a position:* Matte and Jacobs, 10.

- *she did not confine her activities:* Quantz, 4.

- *her boss "was a little reluctant… ":* Matte and Jacobs, 18.

- *established a private law practice:* Quantz, 5.

- *To keep Alfred busy, Loretta gave him:* Interview, Alfred Cox.

- *The next secretarial help:* Matte and Jacobs, 12–13.

- *Loretta said they "almost starved to death":* Quantz, 5.

- *She represented District 18:* "Miss Lorna Lockwood Seeks Re-election to Legislature," *Arizona Republic*, October 5, 1940.

- *Lorna and another legislator... spoke:* "Civil Service Bill is Meeting Topic," *Arizona Republic*, February 20, 1939.

- *"to the greatest degree consistent":* "Lorna E. Lockwood to Seek Re-election," *Phoenix Gazette*, September 5, 1940.

- *she produced thirteen bills:* Quantz, 5.

- *creation of a new state board of health:* Peplow, vol. II, 44.

- *She served on several committees:* J. Morris Richards, "History of the Arizona Legislature, 1912–1967," (unpublished manuscript, 1990), 524–525.

- *"The feminine legislator rapidly acquired":* "Lorna Lockwood To Be Honored," *Mesa Tribune*, September 10, 1975.

- *Lorna was one of seventy-five women:* "Parley Calls Local Woman," *Arizona Republic*, January 3, 1940.

- *Lorna returned to Washington as the assistant:* Quantz, 5; "Arizonans in Washington," *Arizona Daily Star*, January 19, 1942.

- *"I...want to thank someone for this Arizona sunshine":* Matte and Jacobs, 15.

- *Mrs. Murdock took Lorna: Ibid.,* 15–16.

- *Admission to practice law before the United States Supreme Court:* http://www.supremecourt.gov/bar/barinstructions.pdf

- *She said she also "learned a lot about Congress":* Matte and Jacobs, 19.

- *which she called "the best state":* Duffy.

- *her childhood goal, going into private law practice:* Kiel.

- *in the firm of Cox, Lockwood, and Lockwood: Arizona State Legislature: Biographical information forms,* January 31, 1939 and January 14, 1947, Phoenix, AZ: Arizona State Library, Archives, and Public Records.

- *She had a standing lunch reservation:* Interview, Alan Cox.

- *"We used to network," attorney Virginia Hash stated:* Interview, Virginia Hash, transcript.

- *"I remember walking into court":* Ibid.

- *"the darndest fluorescent socks":* Ibid.

- *"you never crowed."* Ibid.

- *she was appointed assistant attorney general:* Interview, Edward Jacobson.

- *That same year, Attorney General Fred O. Wilson:* Ibid.

- *During one of these parties Lorna announced:* Ibid.

- *She was already a member of the board:* "Lorna E. Lockwood Heading for Bench."

- *"If you're going to be a judge":* Interview, Virginia Hash, transcript.

- *"I know most of you have already decided":* Interview, Alan Cox.

- *but the voters granted her request:* "Croaff Takes Position in Contest For Superior Bench," *Phoenix Gazette,* September 13, 1950.

- *"I believed when I decided to run for judge"* "Lorna E. Lockwood Heading For Bench."

- *Lorna's upset victory gave Arizona:* "Lorna E. Lockwood, Struckmeyer Strong As Bernstein Trails," *Phoenix Gazette,* September 13, 1950.

Chapter Three: Lady Law

- *"I remember the first day she was on the bench":* Interview, Virginia Hash, transcript.

- *"She's going to do all right":* Interview, Alfred and Alan Cox.

- *Alfred died a few months later.* Ibid

- *If Virginia's first impression of Lorna": Interview,* Mark Harrison.

- *"I decided that I would run the court,"* Matte and Jacobs, 22–23

- *there were two...rather prominent lawyers:* Earl Zarbin, *The Bench and the Bar: A History of Maricopa County's Legal Professions* (Chatsworth, California: Windsor Publications, Inc., 1991).

- *Lorna was tested by a young man:* Interview, Alfred Cox.

- *"She later reversed her decision":* Hutton, Ginger. "50 years balancing scales of justice: Her Honor remembers..." *Arizona Republic* (Phoenix, AZ), July 20, 1975.

- *"The jury found the defendant not guilty and I was furious":* Ibid.

- *knew when to temper justice with mercy:* Kiel.

- *"A couple phoned me about 10:00 one evening":* "Ambitious Lorna Lockwood Holds Title of First Woman Judge in the State," *Arizona Daily Star*, January 13, 1952.

- *One of the most important things:* Kiel.

- *"I have a very strong feeling":* Duffy.

- *after Lorna became a judge, she was invited:* "More Interest In Law Needed."

- *Lorna had an interest in adoption laws:* Telephone interview, Walter Cheifitz.

- *led her, finally, to the juvenile court:* Matte and Jacobs, 26–27.

- *Lorna achieved statewide fame:* "Lorna Lockwood dies, retired Arizona justice," *Arizona Republic,* September 24, 1977.

- *that this would "result in helpful suggestions":* Kiel.

- *"I've seen working, widowed mothers":* Ibid.

- *"without this closeness there is apt to be trouble":* Duffy.

- *"It's obvious the child is starved for love":* Kiel.

- *led Lorna to establish:* Matte and Jacobs, 26–27.

- *she did not think harsh retribution:* Kiel.

- *"A long sentence merely embitters the person":* Hutton.

- *"If you don't straighten out your life":* Story told to the author's husband, Richard David, by an anonymous woman who visited the author's and her husband's Lorna Lockwood exhibit at the State Capitol on February 14, 2011.

- *"You did something to me":* Hutton.

- *Although Lorna was an outstanding:* Kiel.

- *"just be yourself and be a lawyer":* Ibid.

- *a woman who wanted to be a judge:* Interview, Virginia Hash, transcript.

- *Lorna was extremely careful:* Interview, Elizabeth Stover.

- *"She was a great judge, maybe the best":* Interview, John Frank.

- *The Supreme Court's Miranda decision:* Zarbin, 73.

Chapter Four: Smooth Moves

- *She loved to read:* Duffy.

- *She loved her garden:* Matte and Jacobs, 35.

- *One of those was:* Interview, Virginia Hash, transcript.

- *Lorna loved opera:* Matte and Jacobs, 35.

- *When in the late 1940s:* Interview, Floyd Denton.

- *While adults often found Lorna somewhat intimidating:* Telephone interview, Stirley Cantor.

- *Lorna was devoted:* Kiel.

- *"She went out of her way":* Interview, Alfred Cox.

- *Lorna would say, "it would be difficult":* Kiel.

- *In 1960, after Lorna had served:* Interview, Alan Cox.

- *she had not always been a good public speaker:* Interview, Virginia Hash, transcript.

- *just as she did in the courtroom:* "Ambitious Lorna Lockwood..."

- *Virginia Hash flew Lorna all over the state:* Interview, Mary Schroeder.

- *Lorna was terrified the first time she flew:* Matte and Jacobs, 37–38.

- *Virginia recalled some "rare adventures":* Interview, Virginia Hash, transcript.

- *Lorna was "furious" with her team:* Ibid.

- *Below is an excerpt:* Matte and Jacobs, 32.

- *Lorna's nieces and nephews began:* Interview, Alan Cox.

- *Lorna was acting on the advice:* Angele Solano, "Lorna Lockwood: Lawyer, Legislator, Leader" (student paper, April 20, 2001), PDF file. http://wlh-static.law.stanford.edu/papers/LockwoodL_Solano01.pdf.

- *On September 13, Rose Mofford, executive secretary:* Primary Election Registration, September 13, 1960 (Phoenix, AZ: Office of the Secretary of State), PDF file. http://www.azsos.gov/election/VoterReg/History/Source/Primary/1960.pdf.

- *John Frank... cheered Lorna on:* Interview, John Frank.

Chapter Five: You've Come a Long Way, Baby

- *"Lady, you can't park there!":* Matte and Jacobs, 44; Hutton.

- *In the presence of the other four justices:* Interview, Alfred Cox.

- *she entered her father's old office:* "Lorna Lockwood is Chief Justice," *Phoenix Gazette*, January 7, 1965.

- *"I cannot fill my father's shoes":* Kiel.

- *The supreme court, which consists of five people:* "How a Case Moves Through the Court System," *Guide to Arizona Courts.* http://www.azcourts.gov/guidetoazcourts/HowaCase MovesThroughtheCourtSystem.aspx.

- *Mark Harrison, who had graduated:* Interview, Mark Harrison.

- *that she wrote the court's unanimous ruling:* Harrison, *Arizona State Law Journal.*

- *She quoted the U.S. Supreme Court decision:* Ibid.

- *She wrote the dissent in State v. Taylor:* Solano, 16.

- *One law she thought was right:* Interview, Alan Cox.

- *She wrote the opinion in what most legal scholars consider:* Copy of *Stone v. Arizona Highway Commission*, copies of the Pima County Superior Court filings, and the medical report provided by Lisa Patton of the Legal Records Department of the Clerk of the Superior Court at the Pima County Court in Tucson. Additional information about *Stone v. Arizona Highway Commission* can be found at http://174.123.24.242/leagle/xmlResult.aspx?xmldoc= 196347793Ariz384_1410.xml&docbase=CSLWAR1- 1950-1985.

- *"It was that old philosophy that the king can do no wrong":* "Retired Justice Lockwood says she favors ERA."

- *"I have always prided myself":* Ibid.

- *her sovereign immunity decision was followed:* Andrews.

- *Shirley v. Superior Court:* Colleen Echeveste, *"Lorna Elizabeth Lockwood: In Pursuit of the 1976 U.S. Supreme Court Nomination" (student paper, January 24, 2003), PDF file, 23. http://wlh-static.law.stanford.edu/papers0203/LockwoodL-Echeveste03.pdf.*

- *"In practicing what she preached":* Andrews.

- *"It's the right thing to do":* Interview, John Frank.

- *"this is the first time in the 189 years":* "Lorna Lockwood is Chief Justice."

- *President Lyndon B. Johnson wrote "I know":* "Lorna Lockwood to be Honored"

- *"This is just about the happiest day of my life":* "New State Chief Justice Keeps Date With History," *Evening American*, January 11, 1965.

- *"I supervise all judges":* Ibid.

- *She was also in charge of setting up:* "Lorna Lockwood Is Chief Justice."

- *Lorna's "devoted and untiring efforts":* Fred Struckmeyer, "Justice Lorna E. Lockwood:

Reflections of a Fellow Jurist," *Arizona State Law Journal,* v–vi.

- *The California chapter of...Women Lawyers:* Matte and Jacobs, 45–55.

- *"no woman is capable of being a judge":* Interview, Alan Cox.

- *Thurgood Marshall, who would become the first African American:* Matte and Jacobs, 55.

- *"I like very much the work I am doing":* Kiel.

- *president of the Phoenix Soroptimist Club:* Duffy.

- *she taught a non-partisan class in politics:* Matte and Jacobs, 30–31.

- *to "seek public office" themselves:* "Lorna Lockwood Is Chief Justice," *Phoenix Gazette,* January 7, 1965.

- *The* Gardner v. Gardner *divorce case:* Quantz, 12.

- *claimed not to be a militant feminist:* Kiel.

- *"I have found during all my professional life":* "New State Chief Justice..."

- *"I had to work twice as hard":* "Retired Justice Lockwood says she favors ERA."

- *She was "an indefatigable campaigner for the ERA":* Interview, Mary Schroeder.

- *those who opposed the ERA "brainwashed":* "Retired Justice Lockwood Says She Favors ERA."

- *before they knew the facts were "downright damaging"*: Kiel.

- *"I can't understand why some women are against it"*: Andrews.

- *Lorna's "red hair glows when she is angered"*: Kiel.

- *the lawyers called her Goldilocks:* Interviews, Alan Cox, Mark Harrison.

- *you had better have a "good sense of humor"*: Solano, 25.

- *merit appointment of judges by the governor:* David Daugherty, "Selecting Our Judges," *Arizona Republic* (Phoenix, AZ) March 27, 2011.

- *Judge Thomas Tang's re-election loss:* Helen Perry Grimwood, in *One Hundred Women and Minority Lawyers* (Phoenix, AZ: Maricopa County Bar Association/State Bar of Arizona, 2000), DVD.

- *"It was easier for women to go into politics"*: Andrews.

- *But now she was seventy-two years old:* Matte and Jacobs, 56.

- *battling diabetes:* Interview, Alan Cox.

- *press conference at the supreme court:* Hutton.

- *"Justice Lorna Lockwood...challenged traditions"*: "A Woman Far Ahead Of The Times," *Phoenix Gazette*, May 15, 1975.

- *"Justice Lockwood's chief contribution to the bench":* "Woman of a Generation," *Arizona Republic*, May 15, 1975.

- *her friends honored her with a banquet:* Interview, Alfred Cox, Alan Cox.

- *"More than 900 persons from across the state":* "Event Salutes Lockwood: Returning to Law Practice," Mesa Tribune, September 22, 1975.

- *Lorna joined her brother-in-law, Simpson Cox, and her nephw, Alfred:* Interview, Alan Cox.

- *After the service, as she walked:* Interview, Alfred Cox, Alan Cox.

- *At the Capitol that morning: In Remembrance,* leaflet from memorial service for Lorna Lockwood, September 27 1977.

- *"Lorna was destined for a legal career":* "Woman of a Generation," *Arizona Republic*, May 15, 1975.

Chapter Six: Lorna's Legacy

- *The doll, called the Lorna Lockwood Memorial:* Interviews, Elizabeth Stover, Mary Schroeder.

- *Author's note:* I first saw the Lorna Lockwood Traveling Memorial Trophy (Judge Barbie) in 2001, in a dark case across from the archives in the Arizona Historical Society Museum in Tempe. I learned something of the trophy's history when I later interviewed the Honorable Elizabeth Stover. Judge Stover told me that when the trophy was given to her it had no pedestal. In 2010 I found the trophy, now prominently displayed, in the Sandra Day O'Connor exhibit in the museum. I learned the whole story of the trophy on August 25 of that year when I interviewed the Honorable Mary Schroeder at the Sandra Day O'Connor Federal Courthouse in Phoenix.

- *the state of New York did not have a woman:* "Chief Judge Is Retiring, Leaving Trail of Successes for Women on the Bench," *New York Times,* December 28, 2008.

- *"Civilization is based upon law and order"*: "More Interest In Law Needed."

- *"Justice Lockwood has always been regarded":* Mark Harrison, "Justice Lorna E. Lockwood: Reflections of Her First Law Clerk," *Arizona State Law Journal* Vol. 1975, Number 1, xi.

- *Origin of Lady Justice:* www.commonlaw.com/Justice.html.

- *Lorna "was the snowplow that broke the path":* Interview, John Frank.

- *"Writer of Many...Beautifully Wrought Opinions":* American Trial Lawyers Association Award of Merit, Cox family collection.

- *"Each position I held in Arizona":* Matte and Jacobs, introduction.

- *five Girl Scouts who grew up to be lawyers:* Helen Perry Grimwood, *One Hundred Women and Minority Lawyers.*

161

Lorna's Awards

- *Arizona Elected Officials: Biographical information form* (Phoenix, AZ: Arizona State Library, Archives, and Public Records), April 18, 1975.

- *One Hundred Women and Minority Lawyers* Awards Program.

∽ BIBLIOGRAPHY ∾

Andrews, Phil. "Decisions of Wisdom," Lockwood
Behest. *Arizona Weekly Gazette* (Phoenix, AZ), October
4, 1977.

Arizona Daily Star (Tucson, AZ):

- "Ambitious Lorna Lockwood Holds Title of First
  Woman Judge in the State." January 13, 1952.

- "Arizonans in Washington." January 19, 1942.

- "More Interest In Law Needed." January 13, 1952.

- "State's First Woman Chief Justice Dies." September
  24, 1977.

Arizona Elected Officials: Biographical information form.
    April 18, 1975. Phoenix, AZ: Arizona State
    Library, Archives, and Public Records.

Arizona Highways. This Month in History. December 2008.

Arizona Republic (Phoenix, AZ):

- "Civil Service Bill Is Meeting Topic." February 20, 1939.

- "Lorna Lockwood dies; retired Arizona justice." September 24, 1977.

- "Miss Lorna Lockwood Seeks Re-Election To Legislature." October 5, 1940.

- "On This Date In Arizona History." May 23, 2011.

- "Parley Calls Local Woman." January 3, 1940.

- "State Bar's Role Keeps Courts Independent." March 27, 2011.

- "Tombstone in Bloom." March 26, 2011.

- "Woman of a Generation." May15, 1975.

Arizona State Legislature: Biographical information forms. January 31, 1939 and January 14, 1947. Phoenix, AZ: Arizona State Library, Archives, and Public Records.

Arizona Women's Hall of Fame Records, 1980–1991. Arizona Historical Society Library and Archives, Central Arizona Division, Tucson, AZ.

Biographical information form: Justice Lorna E. Lockwood. 1975. Phoenix, AZ: Arizona State Library, Archives, and Public Records.

Blackman, Marjorie Freburg. Chi Omega House collection, University of Arizona; author's collection.

Carlson, M. Dosia. Eulogy at memorial service for Charlotte Cox, December 6, 2003.

Cantor, Stirley. Telephone interview. March 8, 2001.

Cheifetz, Walter. Telephone interview. November 26, 2003.

Cox, Alan. Personal interviews. March 1, 2001; May 13 2001; April 15, 2007; February 14 and 19, 2011.

Cox, Alfred. Personal interviews. December 11, 2000; February 14 and 19, 2011.

Cox, Charlotte Lockwood. Personal interview. December 11, 2000.

Daugherty, David B. "Selecting Our Judges." *Arizona Republic* (Phoenix, AZ) March 27, 2011.

David, Sonja White. "Lady Law: The Legacy of Lorna Lockwood." *The Eleusis of Chi Omega* (Fall 2001): 46–47.

Davies, Lynn. *History of the Mexican Revolution.* http://www.ic.arizona.edu/ic/mcbride/ws200/mex-davi.htm.

Denton, Floyd. Personal interview. December 15, 2001.

Denton, Nettie Shreck. Personal interviews. 1945–1954.

Douglas Station. U.S. Customs and Border Protection. Article published September 20, 2010.

http://www.cbp.gov/xp/cgov/border_security/bord er_patrol/border_patrol_sectors/

tucson_sector_az/stations/douglas.xml.

Duffy, Jean. *"Law Was Her Career Ever Since Age of 10."* Arizona Republic (Phoenix, AZ) September 8, 1966.

Echeveste, Colleen. "Lorna Elizabeth Lockwood: In Pursuit of the 1976 U.S. Supreme Court Nomination." Student paper, January 24, 2003. PDF file. http://wlh-static.law.stanford.edu/papers 0203/LockwoodL-Echeveste03.pdf.

Evening American (Phoenix, AZ). "New State Chief Justice Keeps Date With History." January 11, 1965.

Frank, John:

- "Justice Lorna E. Lockwood: Reflections of an Appellate Attorney." *Arizona State Law Journal* 1975, no. 1.

- Personal interview. April 3, 2001.

Gartell, Barry, ed. *Times Past: Reflections from Arizona History.* Phoenix, AZ: Arizona Capitol Times, 2008.

Harrison, Mark I.:

- "Justice Lorna E. Lockwood: Reflections of Her First Law Clerk." *Arizona State Law Journal* Vol. 1975, Number 1.

- Personal interview. May 27, 2008.

Harvill, Richard. Letter to Lorna Lockwood. Cox family collection.

Hash, Virginia. Interview for the Evo De Concini Oral History Project. *Arizona Legal History Project.* Arizona Historical Society Library and Archives, Central Arizona Division, Tucson, AZ.

Haunts and History. http//www.hotelgadsden.com/hotel.html.

"Her Honor Takes the Bench." *Time* 85, no. 5 (January 29,1965), http://www.time.com/time/magazine/article/0,917 1,839164-1,00.html.

"How a Case Moves Through the Court System." *Guide to Arizona Courts.* http://www.azcourts.gov/guidetoazcourts/HowaCa seMovesThroughtheCourtSystem.aspx.

Hutton, Ginger. "50 years balancing scales of justice: Her Honor remembers..." *Arizona Republic* (Phoenix, AZ), July 20, 1975.

In Remembrance. Leaflet from memorial service for Lorna Lockwood, September 27 1977.

Jacobson, Edward. Personal interview. March 27, 2001.

Kiel, Henry R. "Arizona's Chief Supreme Court Justice." *Arizona Days and Ways Magazine* 25 (April1965).

Mesa (AZ) Tribune:

- "Event Salutes Lockwood; Returning to Law Practice." September 22, 1975.

- "Lorna Lockwood To Be Honored." September 10, 1975.

Malatin, Jeff. *II: Women in Arizona Politics: From Suffrage to Governing*. Arizona Women and Politics. http://www.ic.arizona.edu/ic/mcbride/ws200/pol.htm.

Marcovitz, Hal. *Pancho Villa*. Philadelphia: Chelsea House, 2002.

Matte, Nancy L. and Jacobs, Thomas A. "Justice Was a Lady: A Biography of the Public Life of Lorna E. Lockwood." Unpublished manuscript, 1985.

Mofford, Rose. Telephone interview. September 15, 2009.

Morton, Wendy, director. *Legends of the Judiciary: A Video Retrospective on Arizona's Proud Judicial Tradition*. Phoenix, AZ: Arizona Supreme Court, 2010. http://www.azcourts.gov/educationservices/COJETClassroom/VideoCenter/LegendsoftheJudiciary.aspx.

New York Times. "Chief Judge Is Retiring, Leaving Trail of Successes for Women on the Bench." December 28, 2008.

Norvelle, Astrid. Law Library, James E. Rogers College of Law, University of Arizona. E-mail communications. September 1, 2009-October 12, 2011.

Old Tombstone: www.discoverseaz.com

One Hundred Women and Minority Lawyers. Phoenix, AZ: Maricopa County Bar Association/State Bar of Arizona, 2000. DVD, print.

Origin of Lady of Justice. http://www.commonlaw.com/Justice.html.

Panchyk, Richard. *Our Supreme Court: A History with 14 Activities.* Chicago: Chicago Review Press, 2006.

Peplow, Edward H., Jr. *History of Arizona, Vols. I and II.* New York: Lewis Historical Publishing Co. Inc., 1958.

Phoenix (AZ) Gazette:

- "A Woman Far Ahead Of The Times." May 15, 1975.

- "Croaff Takes Fifth Position in Contest For Superior Bench." September 13, 1950. Late edition.

- "Lorna E. Lockwood, Heading For Bench, Is About To Realize A Lifelong Ambition." September 13, 1950. First edition.

- "Lorna E. Lockwood, Struckmeyer Strong As Bernstein Trails." September 13, 1950. Early edition.

- "Lorna E. Lockwood To Seek Re-election To Legislature." September 5, 1940.

- "Lorna Lockwood Is Chief Justice." January 7, 1965.

- "Retired Justice Lockwood Says She Favors ERA." September 18, 1975.

Pollock, Paul W. "Justice Lorna E. Lockwood." Vol. 1 of *American Biographical Encyclopedia: Profiles of*

Prominent Personalities. Arizona ed. Phoenix, AZ: P.W. Pollock, 1967.

Primary Election Registration, September 13, 1960. Phoenix, AZ: Office of the Secretary of State. PDF file. http://www.azsos.gov/election/VoterReg/History/Source/Primary/1960.pdf.

Quantz, David M. "Lorna Lockwood: A Dynamic Woman in Changing Times." Unpublished manuscript, 1986.

Reidhead, S.J. "Life in 1881 Tombstone, Arizona (blog entry)." *Blogcritics Culture.* Last modified October 8, 2006. http://blogcritics.org/culture/article/life-in-1881-tombstone-arizona.

Richards, J. Morris. "History of the Arizona Legislature, 1912–1967." Unpublished manuscript, 1990.

Schroeder, Mary M. Personal interview. August 25, 2010.

Solano, Angele C. "Lorna Lockwood: Lawyer, Legislator, Leader." Student paper, April 20, 2001. PDF file. http://wlh-static.law.stanford.edu/papers/LockwoodL_Solano01.pdf.

Stein, R. Conrad. *Pancho Villa: Mexican Revolutionary Hero.* Chanhassen, MN: The Child's World, 2004.

Stone v. Arizona Highway Commission. 93 Ariz. 384, 381.P. 2d 107 (Arizona Supreme Court, En Banc, 1963). http://174.123.24.242/leagle/xmlResult.aspx?xmld

oc=196347793Ariz384_1410.xml&docbase=CSL WAR1-1950-1985.

Stover, Elizabeth. Personal interview. February 3, 2001.

Struckmeyer, Fred C. Jr. *"Justice Lorna E. Lockwood: Reflections of a Fellow Jurist." State Law Journal* Vol. 1975, No. 1.

The City of Tombstone's Official Website. "Tombstone, Arizona."http://www.cityoftombstone.com. March 8, 2011.

The Equal Rights Amendment. http://www.equalrightsamendment.org/. May 5, 2011.

The Last of the Grand Hotels. http//www.hotelgadsden.com/hotel.html.

Tinker v. Des Moines Independent Community School District, 393 U.S. 503 (U.S. Supreme Court, 1969). http://www.oyez.org/cases/1960-1969/1968/1968_21.

Tombstone (AZ) Epitaph. "Tombstone Girl Honor Candidate of Phi Kappa Phi." April 1, 1923.

Zarbin, Earl. *The Bench and the Bar: A History of Maricopa County's Legal Professions.* Chatsworth, California: Windsor Publications, Inc., 1991.